What's Your Opinion?

Adams 12 Five Star Schools
1500 E 128th Ave
Thornton, CO 80241
720-972-4000

Grades 6–8

What's Your Opinion?

Richard G. Cote & Darcy O. Blauvelt

PRUFROCK PRESS INC.
WACO, TEXAS

Copyright ©2011 Prufrock Press Inc.

Edited by Sarah Morrison

Production Design by Raquel Trevino

ISBN-13: 978-1-59363-709-5

At the time of this book's publication, all facts and figures cited are the most current available; all telephone numbers, addresses, and website URLs are accurate and active; all publications, organizations, websites, and other resources exist as described in this book; and all have been verified. The authors and Prufrock Press make no warranty or guarantee concerning the information and materials given out by organizations or content found at websites, and we are not responsible for any changes that occur after this book's publication. If you find an error or believe that a resource listed here is not as described, please contact Prufrock Press.

Prufrock Press Inc.
P.O. Box 8813
Waco, TX 76714-8813
Phone: (800) 998-2208
Fax: (800) 240-0333
http://www.prufrock.com

400635970

Table of Contents

Introduction

Background

Gifted program directors, resource specialists, and—perhaps most importantly—general education classroom teachers who struggle with the challenge of providing appropriate services to students of high potential in the traditional classroom may be interested in these Interactive Discovery-Based Units for High-Ability Learners. The units encourage students to use nontraditional methods to demonstrate learning.

Any given curriculum is composed of two distinct, though not separate, entities: content and context. In every classroom environment, there are forces at work that define the content to be taught. These forces may take the form of high-stakes tests or local standards. But in these Interactive Discovery-Based Units for High-Ability Learners, the context of a traditional classroom is reconfigured so that students are provided with a platform from which to demonstrate academic performance and understanding that are not shown through traditional paper-and-pencil methods. This way, teachers go home smiling and students go home tired at the end of the school day.

C = C + C
Curriculum = Content + Context

In March of 2005, the Further Steps Forward Project (FSFP) was established and funded under the Jacob K. Javits Gifted and Talented Students Education Program legislation. The project had a two-fold, long-range mission:

- The first goal was to identify, develop, and test identification instruments specific to special populations of the gifted, focusing on the economically disadvantaged.
- The second goal was to create, deliver, and promote professional development focused on minority and underserved populations of the gifted, especially the economically disadvantaged.

The result was the Student Context Rubric (SCR), which is included in each of the series' eight units. The SCR, discussed in further depth in the Appendix, is a rubric that a teacher or specialist uses to evaluate a student in five areas: engagement, creativity, synthesis, interpersonal ability, and verbal communication. When used in conjunction with the units in this series, the SCR provides specialists with an excellent tool for identifying students of masked potential—students who are gifted but are not usually recognized—and it gives general education teachers the language necessary to advocate for these students when making recommendations for gifted and additional services. The SCR also provides any teacher with a tool for monitoring and better understanding student behaviors.

Using best practices from the field of gifted education as a backdrop, we viewed students through the lens of the following core beliefs as we developed each unit:

- instrumentation must be flexible in order to recognize a variety of potentials;
- curricula must exist that benefit all students while also making clear which students would benefit from additional services; and
- identification processes and services provided by gifted programming must be integral to the existing curriculum; general education teachers cannot view interventions and advocacy as optional.

These eight contextually grounded units, two in each of the four core content areas (language arts, social studies, math, and science), were developed to serve as platforms from which middle school students could strut their stuff, displaying their knowledge and learning in practical, fun contexts. Two of the units (*Ecopolis* and *What's Your Opinion?*) were awarded the prestigious National Association for Gifted Children (NAGC) Curriculum Award in 2009. Over the span of 3 years, we—and other general education teachers—taught all of the units multiple times to measure their effectiveness as educational vehicles and to facilitate dynamic professional development experiences.

The FSFP documented that in 11 of 12 cases piloted in the 2008–2009 school year, middle school students showed statistically significant academic gains. In particular, those students who were underperforming in the classroom showed great progress. Furthermore, there were statistically significant improvements in students' perceptions of their classroom environments in terms of innovation and involvement. Finally, the contextually grounded units in this series can be used as springboards for further study and projects, offering teachers opportunities for cross-disciplinary collaboration.

Administrators, teachers, and gifted specialists will gain from this series a better sense of how to develop and use contextualized units—not only in the regular education classroom, but also in gifted programming.

How to Use the Units

Every lesson in the units includes an introductory section listing the concepts covered, suggested materials, grade-level expectations, and student objectives. This section also explains how the lesson is introduced, how students demonstrate recognition of the concepts, how they apply their knowledge, and how they solve related problems. The lesson plans provided, while thorough, also allow for differentiation and adaptation. Depending on how much introduction and review of the material students need, you may find that some lessons take more or less time than described. We have used these units in 50-minute class periods, but the subparts of the lesson—introducing the material, recognizing the concepts, applying knowledge, and solving a problem—allow for adaptability in terms of scheduling. The "Additional Notes" for each lesson provide further tips, flag potential problem areas, and offer suggestions for extending the lesson.

This series offers many contextual units from which to choose; however, we do not recommend using them exclusively. In our research, we have found that students who are constantly involved in contextual learning become immune to its benefits. We recommend, therefore, that you vary the delivery style of material across the school year. For most classes, spacing out three contextual units over the course of the year produces optimal results.

These units may be used in place of other curriculum. However, if you find that your students are stumbling over a specific skill as they progress through a unit, do not hesitate to take a day off from the unit and instead use direct instruction to teach that skill. This will help to ensure that students are successful as they move forward. It is necessary for students to be frustrated and challenged, as this frustration serves as the impetus of learning—yet they must not be so frustrated that they give up. Throughout the unit, you must find the delicate balance between providing challenges for your students and overwhelming them.

The Role of the Teacher

A contextual unit is a useful vehicle both for engaging your students and for assessing their abilities. As a teacher, your role changes in a contextual unit. Rather than being the driving force, you are the behind-the-scenes producer. The students are the drivers of this creative vehicle. If you are used to direct instruction methods of teaching, you will need to make a conscious choice not to run the show. Although this may feel a bit uncomfortable for you in the beginning, the rewards for your students will prove well worth the effort. As you become more comfortable with the process, you will find that this teaching method is conducive to heightening student engagement and learning while also allowing you to step back and observe your students at work.

Group Dynamics

Cooperation plays a key role in this unit. Small-group work is fraught with challenges for all of us. Creating groups that will be able to accomplish their objectives—groups whose members will fulfill their roles—takes some forethought. Keep in mind that sometimes the very act of working through any issues that arise may be the most powerful learning tool of all. Before beginning the unit, you should discuss with students the importance of working together and assigning tasks to ensure that work is distributed and completed fairly and equally.

Preparation and Pacing

Deciding on a timeline is very important as you plan the implementation of the unit. You know your students better than anyone else does. Some students may be more successful when they are immersed in the unit, running it every day for 3 weeks. Others would benefit from having some days off to get the most out of their experiences.

Every classroom is different. Students possess different sets of prior knowledge, learning strategies, and patterns. This means that as the teacher you must make decisions about how much of the material you will introduce prior to the unit, whether you will provide occasional traditional instruction throughout the unit, how many days off you will give students, and how much your students will discover on their own throughout the course of the unit. For example, in this language arts unit, students need to conduct research to back up their arguments. You can facilitate this research in various ways. You might employ prior projects for which students used research methods; you might have students take notes on research and require them to cite sources appropriately; or you might choose to use the resources provided, directing students to research and defend assigned topics and viewpoints. This book is not meant to provide exact instructions; in every lesson, there is wiggle room in terms of how you work alongside students to enable them to demonstrate their learning.

Also, you should feel free to use materials other than those suggested. If there is a topic or source that is highly relevant for your students, then it might be worthwhile for you to compile research sites, articles, and other materials about the topic in order to provide your students a degree of real-world involvement.

Using these units is a bit like using a recipe in the kitchen. The first time you use one of the units, you may want to use it just as it is written. Each successive time you use it, however, you may choose to adjust the ratios and substitute ingredients to suit your own tastes. The more you personalize the units to your students' situations and preferences, the more engaged they will be—and the same goes for you as the teacher.

Grade-Level Expectations

All of our units are aligned with New Hampshire's Grade-Level Expectations. These state requirements are similar to many states' GLEs, and we hope that they will be useful for you. For each lesson, we have listed the applicable New Hampshire GLEs in a format that illustrates which learning objectives students are meeting by completing the given tasks.

Adaptability

"Organized chaos" is a phrase often used to describe a contextual classroom. The students are not sitting at their desks and quietly taking notes while the teacher delivers information verbally. A classroom full of students actively engaged in their learning and creatively solving real-world problems is messy, but highly productive. Every teacher has his or her own level of tolerance for this type of chaos, and you may find yourself needing days off occasionally. Organization is an essential ingredient for success in a contextual unit. For example, you will need a place in your classroom where students can access paperwork. It is important to think through timeframes and allow for regular debriefing sessions.

You will also want to develop a personalized method for keeping track of who is doing what. Some students will be engaged from the start, but others you will need to prod and encourage to become involved. This will be especially true if your students are unfamiliar with this type of contextual learning. There are always a few students who try to become invisible so that classmates will do their work for them. Others may be Tom Sawyers, demonstrating their interpersonal skills by persuading peers to complete their work. You will want to keep tabs on both of these types of students so that you can maximize individual student learning. Some teachers have students keep journals, others use daily exit card strategies, and others use checklists. Again, many aspects of how to use these units are up to you.

It is difficult in a busy classroom to collect detailed behavioral data about your students, but one advantage of contextual learning is that it is much easier to spend observation time in the classroom when you are not directly running the show! If you have the luxury of having an assistant or classroom visitor who can help you collect anecdotal data, then we recommend keeping some sort of log of student behavior. What has worked well for us has been to create a list of students' pictures, with a blank box next to each picture in which behaviors can be recorded.

Contextual units require the teacher to do a considerable amount of work prior to beginning the unit, but once you have put everything into place, the students take over and you can step back and observe as they work, solve problems, and learn.

Unit Overview

This unit was originally designed in conjunction with the authentic performance assessment of the same title developed by Dr. Tonya Moon, Dr. Carolyn Callahan, Dr. Catherine Brighton, and Dr. Carol Tomlinson under the auspices of the National Research Center on the Gifted and Talented. It should be noted that the original unit focused on persuasive writing, while this adaptation is designed to highlight persuasive speaking. Students are introduced to the elements of making an argument, refuting an argument, and thinking on their feet.

The unit begins by introducing the importance of word choice. The elements of debate, including assertions, reasoning, evidence, conclusions, and fallacies, are illustrated in Lesson 3 by staging a scavenger hunt. The argument puzzle is mastered through an improvisation game that has students use the components of refutation: the opponent's assertion ("They say . . . "), the debater's assertion ("But . . . "), the debater's reasoning and evidence ("Because . . . "), and the debater's conclusion ("Therefore . . . ").

In the final segment, students are assigned topics, sides, and characters to role-play. They are given the prompt for the authentic performance assessment, a debate on one of several teacher-assigned topics. Students conduct research and stage their own debates, taking on their assigned characters' points of view and demonstrating their knowledge of debate structure and effective argumentation.

Unit Outline

We designed these lessons to be used during 50-minute class periods. Depending on the extent to which you need to review concepts with your students, and on the amount of time you decide to devote to particular activities, each of these lessons should take 1–3 days. Lesson 8, during which students research their assigned debate topics, will likely take several additional days, particularly if you decide to give students a lot of freedom regarding topics and characters.

Lesson 1

Students demonstrate their ability to defend an opinion by sustaining arguments with partners. Students are assessed both on their ability to think quickly and on their ability to work with others to sustain an argument. This lesson provides the teacher with an opportunity to preassess the students.

Lesson 2

Students demonstrate their ability to make strong word choices by "translating" statements using a word bank. Students are assessed on their ability to reframe word choices and to evaluate others' choices.

Lesson 3

Students demonstrate their understanding of argumentation concepts (including assertions, reasoning, evidence, fallacies of reasoning, and conclusions) by completing a scavenger hunt. Students are assessed on their ability to complete the Scavenger Hunt sheets.

Lesson 4

Students demonstrate their understanding of refutation by participating in an improvisation game using the four steps of refutation (i.e., hearing an opponent's assertion, countering with one's own assertion, providing reasoning/evidence, and drawing a conclusion). Students are assessed on their team contributions and on their mastery of the information.

Lesson 5

Students demonstrate their understanding of refutation by completing the Deduce the Reasoning sheet. Students are assessed on their ability to problem solve and mount oral defenses of their choices.

Lesson 6

Students demonstrate their understanding of the differences between evidence and opinion and of the concept of a stakeholder in an argument by participating in an impromptu class debate and a subsequent debriefing. Students are assigned topics and characters for the final debates, and they begin investigating their characters' points of view on their assigned topics.

Lesson 7

After reviewing the rubric for the authentic performance assessment, students begin research for the debates, demonstrating an understanding of the parts of an argument by completing either the provided argument cards or the provided outlines. Students are encouraged to anticipate what their opponents might say in the debate so that they can be sure to have evidence with which to refute their opponents' arguments.

Lesson 8

Students complete the research and learn to cite sources completely and according to a specific style. (You can decide whether they use the provided style guide or adhere to a different style, particularly if your school uses a standard style guide.)

Lesson 9

Students demonstrate their ability to synthesize and organize research while working in a group to present a "united front" for the upcoming debates. Each team meets with the teacher to review its work to date.

This unit culminates with debate days that allow pairs of teams to stage their debates. Students are assessed utilizing the authentic performance assessment rubric. Students, on this same day or later on, take the pretest again to serve as a posttest.

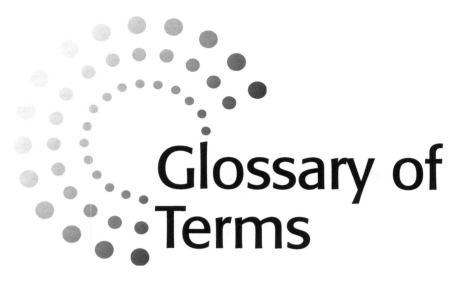

Glossary of Terms

For the purposes of this unit, the following definitions will be used:

- **Analogy:** a comparison between two people, places, events, or ideas
- **Argument:** proof that someone offers to support a belief or statement
- **Assertion:** a clearly stated claim or belief
- **Cause and Effect:** an instance of why something happens and what the result is
- **Conclusion:** a statement that summarizes the argument
- **Constructive Criticism:** the art of giving and receiving nonjudgmental, helpful feedback
- **Costs vs. Benefits:** evaluating an action according to whether it causes more harm than good
- **Debate:** a coherent series of statements beginning with an assertion and leading to a conclusion
- **Evidence:** proof of reasoning
- **Example:** an illustration of the debate issue and an explanation of how it has been resolved in the past
- **Fallacies:** pitfalls or mistakes in reasoning that result in an unsound argument
- **Give and Take:** when each party gives information and listens to the opposition's information in order to respond appropriately; a necessity in any healthy argument
- **Opposition:** a statement that disagrees with the prompt or topic; the con side of the issue
- **Pace:** the speed at which a person speaks
- **Projection:** the ability to speak at a volume appropriate for being heard
- **Proposition:** a statement that agrees with the prompt or topic; the pro side of the issue
- **Reasoning:** a person's explanation for his or her belief or statement
- **Refutation:** an argument or evidence used to prove that another argument, belief, or statement is wrong

Lesson 1

Concepts

- Constructive criticism
- Projecting
- Using appropriate pacing
- Give and take

Materials

- Prewriting Activity sheet (p. 18)
- Argument Game Topics sheet (p. 19)
- Dilemma sheet (pp. 20–21)
- Pretest/posttest rubric (p. 22)

Student Objective

The student demonstrates his or her ability to defend an opinion by sustaining an argument with a peer.

Introduction

Students complete the Prewriting Activity sheet to assess their prior knowledge. (Note that this same sheet will be used as a posttest at the end of the unit.) Work with students to introduce or review the concepts of constructive criticism, projection, pace, and give and take.

Recognition

Working with a volunteer student, demonstrate these concepts by role-playing an argument. You should deliberately offer both positive and negative examples of projection, pace, and give and take. Then, have students use constructive criticism to respond to the demonstration.

Application

Students play a game to demonstrate the importance of thinking quickly and creating a solid argument. The goal of this game is to keep the argument going for as long as possible.

1. Split the group in half. Line up the two groups so that the heads of the line are facing one another. (It doesn't matter whether the group is in one long line or two parallel lines.) Stand between these two students.
2. Inform students that the people they are paired with are their partners, not their opponents.
3. Outline the rules. Make it clear that the point is for students to defend a position, not necessarily to argue their personal convictions.
4. Select and name a topic (e.g., chocolate).
5. Whichever student speaks first can select whether he or she will represent the pro or the con side (e.g., will represent either the benefits or the pitfalls of chocolate).
6. Each student offers reasons supporting his or her point of view. (You may need to moderate this technique so that the debate does not become merely a back-and-forth argument of "Yes, it is" and "No, it isn't.")
7. Call time when the argument falters or when the 2-minute time limit is reached.
8. The students take turns, in pairs, participating in the argument game. After one pair is finished, the two students should go to the ends of their respective lines, and the next pair of students should step up.

As an optional variation on this game, students may work in pairs to practice their technique before they "argue" in front of the class.

Problem Solving

1. Distribute the Dilemma sheet to students and review the instructions. (Students are to list items that they would take on a space shuttle.)
2. Stress the importance of providing justification for the items to be taken on the space voyage.
3. Place students in small groups based on the similarity of their answers.
4. Each group should brainstorm one final list and defend its list to the class.

Grade-Level Expectations

The student:
- Uses varied sentence length and structure.
- States and maintains a focus, a firm judgment, or a point of view when responding to a given question.

- Exhibits logical organization and uses language appropriate for audience, context, and purpose.
- Includes smooth transitions, supports thesis with well-chosen details, and provides a coherent conclusion.
- Uses a variety of strategies of address (e.g., eye contact, speaking rate, volume, articulation, inflection, intonation, rhythm, gesture).

Additional Notes

- For the prewriting activity, you may have students brainstorm everything they know about the topic and write it down. The purpose is to encourage students to activate their prior knowledge, and also to provide you with a preassessment by which to measure academic outcomes.
- The game produces a high level of engagement in most groups, but it may take a few rounds to catch on. Be sure to have a couple of students with stronger verbal skills lead off to model behavior. This activity often becomes a favorite game to play when there is extra time in future classes.
- It is important to keep the game moving. Allow your students some time to think through dead ends (i.e., to identify arguments that cannot be sustained), but not too much time! Call time and quickly move on to the next pair of students to avoid getting bogged down and losing your class's attention.
- Use the suggested topics if desired, or select topics more personal to your class in which students have a vested interest. The suggested topics are formatted as a handout in case you wish to have students free write, brainstorm, or come up with their own topics in advance. It is important to remind students that they may need to defend points of view that are not their own!
- On the scoring rubric, 15 points are possible for correctly describing the order of the debate. You may decide the exact breakdown of how you award these points to students, but it is useful to think of the assertion (pro or con statement), evidence and reasoning, and conclusion as three parts, each worth 5 points. Likewise, it is up to you what criteria to use for awarding the 5 points for organization, style, grammar, and mechanics.

PREWRITING ACTIVITY

Write everything you know about what is included in a debate and the order in which a debate takes place in the space below or on another piece of paper. Use as many of the following words as you can.

Analogy	Argument	Assertion
Cause and effect	Conclusion	Cost and benefits
Debate	Evidence	Example
Fallacies	Give and take	Opposition
Proposition	Reasoning	Refutation

A debate is . . . _____

_____

_____

_____

_____

_____

_____

_____

_____

_____

_____

_____

_____

_____

_____

Name:_____ Date: _____

ARGUMENT GAME TOPICS

Chocolate	School vacation
Year-round school	Homework
School uniforms	High heels
Football	Reading
Cats	Dogs
Ballet	Buses
Spinach	First day of school
Report cards	Science
Projects	Tests
Book reports	Field trips
Cafeteria food	Bake sales
Frogs	Snakes
Television	IMAX movies
MySpace and Facebook	Videogames
Curfew	Graffiti
Detention	American Idol
Pep rallies	Jeans

Name: _____ Date: _____

DILEMMA

You have just received word that you will be one of 12 civilian passengers on a space shuttle to a newly discovered planet. The planet has been found to be ideal for human life. NASA will provide clothing and food for the expedition.

The problem is that the storage space in the shuttle is very small. You may only take 10 items for your personal use. Knowing that you may never return to Earth, what would you take? **Why?**

1. Item you would take: _____

   Why would you take this item? _____

   _____

   _____

   _____

2. Item you would take: _____

   Why would you take this item? _____

   _____

   _____

   _____

3. Item you would take: _____

   Why would you take this item? _____

   _____

   _____

   _____

4. Item you would take: _____

   Why would you take this item? _____

   _____

   _____

   _____

What's Your Opinion? © Prufrock Press Inc.

5. Item you would take: _____

    Why would you take this item? _____

    _____

    _____

    _____

6. Item you would take: _____

    Why would you take this item? _____

    _____

    _____

    _____

7. Item you would take: _____

    Why would you take this item? _____

    _____

    _____

    _____

8. Item you would take: _____

    Why would you take this item? _____

    _____

    _____

    _____

9. Item you would take: _____

    Why would you take this item? _____

    _____

    _____

    _____

10. Item you would take: _____

    Why would you take this item? _____

    _____

    _____

    _____

Student: _____

Date: _____

PRETEST/POSTTEST RUBRIC

Analogy	Argument	Assertion
Cause and effect	Conclusion	Cost and benefits
Debate	Evidence	Example
Fallacies	Give and take	Opposition
Proposition	Reasoning	Refutation

Circle the words listed above used correctly by the student.

The student scores 2 points for every word used correctly
(30 points maximum).

Points scored: _____

The student scores points for correctly describing the order of a debate
(15 points maximum).

Points scored: _____

The student scores points for organization, style, grammar, and mechanics
(5 points maximum).

Points scored: _____

Total points (out of 50 maximum): _____

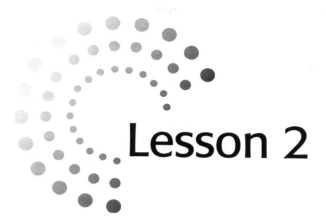

Lesson 2

Concepts

- Writing persuasively
- Framing convincing arguments
- Using constructive criticism

Materials

- List of persuasive words (p. 26)
- List of convincing phrases (p. 27)
- List of statements (p. 28)
- Statement cards (pp. 29–32)
- Scorecards (pp. 33–37)
- Newspaper or Internet article

Student Objective

The student demonstrates his or her ability to make strong word choices by translating and improving statements.

Introduction

Review the uses of persuasive words and convincing phrases, using the provided lists as examples.

Recognition

Give examples of weak- or neutral-language statements by using the provided list of statements. Students, using their lists of persuasive words and convincing phrases as guides, should reframe the given statements into more powerful ones. This can be done individually, in small groups, or as a class.

Application

Students practice strengthening word choice by editing a piece of persuasive text.

1. Either take students to a computer lab or provide a printed editorial column or opinion article to students. If students are working independently online, then they find their own opinion articles that they find interesting (provide guidelines or a list of websites they are allowed to choose from).
2. Students highlight persuasive words and convincing phrases, along with any weak wording, or copy their findings on another sheet of paper.
3. Students then edit sentences, words, and phrases to strengthen the editorial's argument.
4. Remember to have students cite their sources if they find the articles themselves.
5. Have students offer examples to the class of the words and phrases they have edited, or collect their edited samples for your review.

Problem Solving

Students work in teams either to defend or to contest a statement, trying to make their wording and phrasing as convincing as possible.

1. The students are grouped into four teams: two arguing teams, one team that oversees word choice, and one team of judges.
   - **Arguers:** Members of these two teams face one another and begin by defending or contesting the statement as read by the referee (the teacher or an appointed student), who chooses any of the statement cards. Each team can make only one point at a time. Team members should be encouraged to collaborate with one another to reach a team consensus. They may elect to use a spokesperson or take turns representing the group, but everyone should be involved in problem solving.
   - **Word Police:** Members of this team decide whether a statement is worded strongly enough. If they want an arguer to reword a statement, a bell is rung or another appropriate sound is made. The team must then reword the statement in question, using the word list for ideas.
   - **Judges:** At the end of each argument round, the team of judges rates the teams for word choice using the provided scorecards. (Either the judges collaborate on a single score, or each judge offers his or her own individual score.) The judges must be prepared to defend their scores with constructive criticism. (The highest possible score is a 5.)

2. The teacher or appointed referee either pulls a statement from the list or selects a statement card at random, and as with the game in the previous lesson, whichever team speaks first gets to choose its stance.

3. Each round requires two teams to argue, another team to act as the Word Police, and the final team to serve as the Judges.

4. Rounds should be repeated, with teams serving different roles, until students have experienced all roles.

Grade-Level Expectations

The student:

* Connects what has been read to his or her prior knowledge and to other texts by referring to and explaining relevant ideas.
* Exhibits logical organization and uses language appropriate for audience, context, and purpose.
* Selects appropriate words or explains the use of words in context, including content-specific vocabulary, words with multiple meanings, and precise vocabulary.

Additional Notes

* If a visit to the computer lab is possible, have students use an online newspaper article in the application phase. Be sure to have students cite their sources and copy and paste their paragraphs into word documents. This will allow them to mark the text as they read and process the material. In addition to print newspapers and online newspapers, a third option is to distribute a weekly-reader-style current events article, or to select a piece of text that would be particularly relevant for students.
* The problem-solving activity will be a bit shaky at first—loud and boisterous. As the students become more used to the style, they will police themselves.
* Although time is always an issue, we cannot stress enough the importance of having students experience all of the roles in this activity. Students gain a much richer understanding of the importance of word choice by choosing words themselves, watching for word choice in context, and judging the efficacy of different wording.

PERSUASIVE WORDS

Achievement	Appeal
Avoid	Breakthrough
Brilliant	Cautious
Change	Circumstance
Connect	Correlation
Decisive	Deny
Discover	Dominate
Efficient	Essential
Focus	Freedom
Guarantee	Improve
Invasive	Isolate
Justice	Liberty
Motivated	Natural
Organize	Overcome
Prevent	Qualified
Quickly	Recommended
Require	Responsibility
Revolutionary	Sensational
Solve	Specific
Stereotype	Superior
Translation	Truth

What's Your Opinion?

CONVINCING PHRASES

As the evidence shows	Deeply concerned
Bearing in mind	Having considered
Now is the time	Taking into account
The problem with your point of view	For this reason
On the other hand	Many people think
Strongly recommend	Keeping in mind
I suspect that	Without a doubt
Have resolved	Shouldn't we consider
In my opinion	That is the reason why
When you consider that	The truth of the matter
My opponent has said	We must remember

STATEMENTS

Television is a bad influence on children.	The Internet should be free for everyone.
The United States should lower the voting age to 16.	Junk food should be banned in schools.
School should be year-round.	The United States should ban the death penalty.
Students should be allowed to drop out of school after age 12.	Experimental testing on animals should not be allowed.
Homework should be banned.	Schools should provide more social time during the school day.
Dress codes should be mandatory.	Pets should be allowed at schools.
Guns should be illegal for everyone.	Drugs should be legalized so they can be better controlled.
Students should have to learn a foreign language.	Healthcare should be free for everyone.
Snow days should not have to be made up.	Students should have access to soda machines at all times.
The school day should be extended until 6 p.m. every day.	High heels should be allowed in schools.
No animal should be confined to a zoo.	Lacrosse is a better sport than baseball.
Golf is not technically a sport.	Meat is bad for your health.

STATEMENT CARDS

Television is a bad influence on children.

The Internet should be free for everyone.

The United States should lower the voting age to 16.

Junk food should be banned in schools.

School should be year-round.

The United States should ban the death penalty.

What's Your Opinion? © Prufrock Press Inc.

29

Permission is granted to photocopy or reproduce this page for single classroom use only.

STATEMENT CARDS

Students should be allowed to drop out of school after age 12.

Experimental testing on animals should not be allowed.

Homework should be banned.

Schools should provide more social time during the school day.

Dress codes should be mandatory.

Pets should be allowed at schools.

STATEMENT CARDS

Guns should be illegal for everyone.	Drugs should be legalized so they can be better controlled.
Students should have to learn a foreign language.	Healthcare should be free for everyone.
Snow days should not have to be made up.	Students should have access to soda machines at all times.

What's Your Opinion? © Prufrock Press Inc.

Permission is granted to photocopy or reproduce this page for single classroom use only.

31

STATEMENT CARDS

The school day should
be extended until
6 p.m. every day.

High heels should be
allowed in schools.

No animal should be
confined to a zoo.

Lacrosse is a better
sport than baseball.

Golf is not technically
a sport.

Meat is bad for
your health.

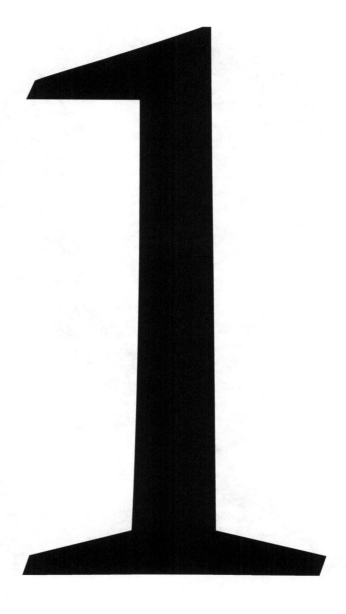

What's Your Opinion? © Prufrock Press Inc.

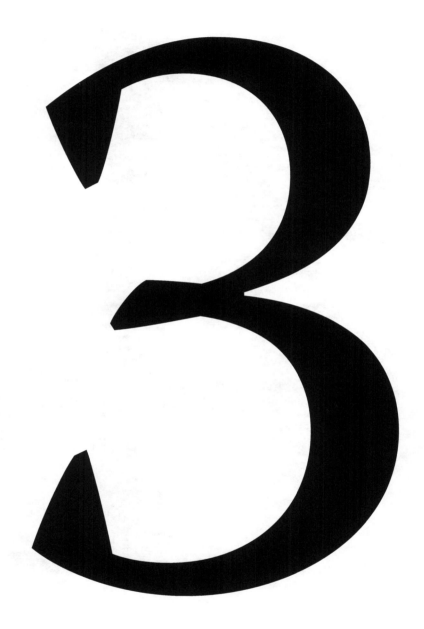

What's Your Opinion? © Prufrock Press Inc.
Permission is granted to photocopy or reproduce this page for single classroom use only.

Lesson 3

Concepts

- Using assertions
- Reasoning
- Using evidence
- Drawing conclusions

Materials

- Posters/visual aids for argument parts (pp. 41–44)
- Scavenger Hunt sheet (pp. 45–46)
- Argument guides (pp. 47–50)
- Parts of argument cards (pp. 51–58)

Student Objective

The student demonstrates an understanding of the parts of an argument by completing a Scavenger Hunt sheet and creating an argument from an assigned point of view.

Introduction

Using the provided visual aids, introduce and discuss the following concepts:
- **Assertion/opening statement:** a clearly stated claim or belief
- **Reasoning:** a person's explanation for his or her belief or statement
- **Evidence:** proof for the explanation
- **Conclusion:** a final statement summarizing what has been said
- **Fallacies:** pitfalls or inconsistencies that weaken reasoning (no visual aid provided)

You can go through several examples of each of these. It should be noted that although no visual aid is provided to illustrate the concept of fallacies, you should discuss fallacies in the context of types of evidence so that students understand how to avoid making fallacious arguments. You might discuss other fallacies in addition to these two, if you wish.

- A **fallacy of division** occurs when a conclusion is based on incorrectly applying a general part of the argument to a specific part (e.g., the average American family has 2.3 children, and the Smith family is an average American family, so the Smith family has 2.3 children).
- A **fallacy of composition** occurs when parts of an argument add up to a whole that does not make sense (e.g., Joe likes fish, and he also likes ice cream, so he will like sardine ice cream).

Post the visual aids in four separate areas of the room, and place the "parts of argument" cards near them.

Recognition

Students should describe each concept verbally. If you like, have students create examples or write paragraphs involving the parts of argument.

Application

Students participate in a scavenger hunt to prove that they understand how arguments are organized.

1. Individual students or small groups receive their Scavenger Hunt sheets.
2. You may choose to assign students topics from those provided (e.g., tell them they are either pro or con on the topic of hunting). If you want to provide an opportunity for more challenge, you can tell them to create their own topics. This will necessitate that they create their own arguments, rather than locating the puzzle pieces (i.e., parts of argument cards) to complete the given arguments.
3. The students complete their scavenger hunt sheets using the appropriate parts of argument. Each student needs to locate the assertion, reasoning, evidence, and conclusion cards that correspond to his or her topic, also ensuring that no fallacies have been used.
4. Students or groups share their completed arguments with the class.
5. Use the provided argument guides to moderate students' discussion.

Problem Solving

Students use their knowledge of the parts of an argument to stage another debate, this one more structured than the impromptu exercises they have been doing.

1. Students brainstorm a list of topics that are pertinent to their lives. This may be done in a small-group format or as a whole-class activity where students raise their hands and the teacher writes all of the ideas on the board.
2. Each small group is assigned either the pro or the con side for one of the topics. (Be sure that if a topic has a pro side, it also has a con side, and vice versa.)
3. The teams put together arguments using the four parts of an argument (i.e., assertion, reasoning, evidence, and conclusion).
4. Students argue their points of view in front of the class and receive constructive criticism from the audience.

Grade-Level Expectations

The student:
*   Evaluates information presented in terms of relevance.
*   Gathers, organizes, analyzes, and interprets the information.
*   Uses evidence to support conclusions.
*   Uses information from the text to answer questions, to state the main/central ideas, or to provide supporting details.
*   Includes smooth transitions, supports his or her thesis with well-chosen details, and provides a coherent conclusion.

Additional Notes

*   To help the more visual learners, we recommend that you color code the parts of argument cards (e.g., assertion cards are red, reasoning cards are blue).
*   Depending on the ability level and resourcefulness of the students, you can choose either to sort out the cards into categories or to mix them into one big pile.
*   It is important that you take adequate time to discuss the concepts at the beginning of the lesson.
*   When students debate on the topics they have brainstormed, please note that this is not intended to be a factual, research-based argument, but rather a role-play to reinforce the concepts of the various parts of an argument. You can moderate this activity in several ways—for instance, you might decide to impose a time limit or to incorporate word choice rules into this exercise, if you think that students could benefit from reviewing those concepts.

ASSERTION

Year-round school is a good idea.

The more books you read, the better your grades in school will be.

Opening statement that clearly makes the claim or states the belief that is to be debated

Cats are more affectionate than dogs are.

It is not healthy to drink soda.

REASONING

Year-round schooling has been linked to higher scholastic achievement.

Verbal SAT scores are directly linked to the average number of hours spent per week reading.

Statement explaining why the audience should believe the assertion

Cats are physically small enough to sit on people's laps, while only some dogs are able to fit on laps.

Sodas contain a high amount of sugar or artificial sweeteners that have been shown to increase body weight.

EVIDENCE

In schools that have year-round classes, achievement scores have risen 20% in 2 years.

Students who read at least 4 hours a week outside of school usually score in the 600–800 range for the verbal section of the SAT.

Proof of the reasoning used to explain an assertion

The average size for a cat in the United States is 8–15 lbs., while the average dog weighs 30 lbs.

Women who increase their consumption of soda from less than one per week to one or more per day gained an average of 10.3 lbs. within 1 year.

CONCLUSION

If a school district wants to raise scholastic achievement, year-round schooling is a good idea.

The amount that a student reads is a strong predictor of how well he or she will do in school.

Statement that summarizes an argument

The size of a cat enables it to be more affectionate than a dog.

People who drink soda every day have a tendency to be overweight.

Name:_____ Date: _____

SCAVENGER HUNT

Your mission is to choose an assertion statement and then build an argument to support it. Find cards that make sense to build your argument, copy down what is on the cards, and put them back so that other people can use them.

1. Assertion (clearly states a claim or belief): _____

_____

_____

_____

_____

_____

_____

_____

_____

_____

2. Reasoning (provides explanation of belief): _____

_____

_____

_____

_____

_____

_____

_____

_____

_____

_____

_____

What's Your Opinion? © Prufrock Press Inc.   45

Permission is granted to photocopy or reproduce this page for single classroom use only.

3. Evidence (provides proof of explanation): _____

    _____

    _____

    _____

    _____

    _____

    _____

    _____

4. Conclusion (summarizes an argument): _____

    _____

    _____

    _____

    _____

    _____

    _____

    _____

5. Have you used the parts of an argument to make a whole? If not, go back and correct your work.

6. Check for fallacies:
    - Is your conclusion based on incorrectly applying a general part of the argument to a specific part? (For example: The average American family has 2.3 children. The Smith family is an average American family. Therefore, the Smith family has 2.3 children.) This is a **fallacy of division.**
    - Have you used parts of an argument to make a whole that doesn't make sense? (For example: Joe likes fish and he likes ice cream, so he will like sardine ice cream.) This is a **fallacy of composition**.

    If your argument contains any fallacies, then you must go back and correct them.

ARGUMENT GUIDE: PETS

	PROPOSITION	OPPOSITION
ASSERTION	People who own pets have lower levels of stress.	Pets only add to the stress levels of their owners.
REASONING	Petting and interacting with animals lowers anxiety and promotes positive thinking.	There is a great deal of work associated with caring for pets (e.g., feeding them, walking them, cleaning up after them).
EVIDENCE	Studies have shown that interacting with cats and dogs lowers blood pressure more effectively than blood pressure medicine does.	The cost of owning a dog over an average lifetime (14 years) can range from $4,000–$40,000!
CONCLUSION	Pet owners are healthier than those who do not own pets due to their interactions with their cats and dogs.	The cost of owning a pet is so high that it greatly increases the level of stress for pet owners.

Name: _____   Date: _____

ARGUMENT GUIDE: HUNTING

	PROPOSITION	OPPOSITION
ASSERTION	Hunting is a time-honored sport.	Hunting is nothing but licensed animal cruelty and should be banned.
REASONING	Hunting animals serves many purposes, including thinning overpopulated animal species and feeding needy families.	There is no sport in tracking down animals with motorized vehicles and shooting them with long-range weapons.
EVIDENCE	A hunter's bullet is far more humane than slow starvation. Thousands of deer starved to death in the winter of 2007 due to harsh conditions. One moose can supply 500 lbs. of meat!	Hunters kill more than 130 million animals in the United States every year. This is a wasteful use of our natural animal resources.
CONCLUSION	Hunting wild animals is a right that all Americans should continue to enjoy.	Hunting is an unethical and cruel activity that is disguised as a sport.

ARGUMENT GUIDE: STUDENT ATHLETES

	PROPOSITION	OPPOSITION
ASSERTION	Student athletes should have to maintain a minimum grade point average.	Academic standing should not interfere with a student's right to participate in sports.
REASONING	Athletics are very worthwhile extracurricular activities; however, academics must remain the focus of a student's work.	Many student athletes depend on athletic achievements to get a scholarship to college. They should not be banned from playing a sport because of a drop in grades.
EVIDENCE	Colleges require athletes to maintain a minimum grade point average. If high schools do not provide their athletes with strong academic backgrounds, then athletic scholarships will not help athletes finish college.	Studies have shown that on average, student athletes perform better than nonathletes in the classroom. If athletes have a minimum grade requirement, then all students who participate in an activity should also have such a requirement.
CONCLUSION	Student athletes must maintain a minimum G.P.A. in order to ensure that their academics do not suffer from their focus on athletics.	Minimum G.P.A. requirements for student athletes are unfair and only serve to promote a negative stereotype.

ARGUMENT GUIDE: SCHOOL PAPERS

	PROPOSITION	OPPOSITION
ASSERTION	School newspapers should not be subject to censorship.	School newspapers report on our schools; therefore, school administrators should have control over what is being published.
REASONING	America prides itself on its Bill of Rights, which includes the freedom of speech. Can we grant our school newspapers anything less?	Middle school and high school students are learning the responsibilities associated with the printed word. They need direction from adults.
EVIDENCE	Historically, censorship has led to an uninformed public. This is very dangerous in a democracy. The school newspaper is one of the few outlets students have to express their views and to inform fellow students.	School administrators have the responsibility to oversee published material to be certain that articles reflect the truth and do not exploit individuals. Parents have sued schools after their children were embarrassed in school newspapers.
CONCLUSION	Freedom of speech is an American right guaranteed by the Constitution. Being a student should not result in being denied that right.	Administrators should approve school newspapers before they go to press. It is the school's job to model responsible behavior.

ASSERTIONS (PRO)

People who own pets have lower levels of stress.

Hunting is a time-honored sport.

Student athletes should have to maintain a minimum grade point average.

School newspapers should not be subject to censorship.

Write your own assertion.

Write your own assertion.

ASSERTIONS (CON)

Pets only add to the stress levels of their owners.

Hunting is nothing but licensed animal cruelty and should be banned.

Academic standing should not interfere with a student's right to participate in sports.

School newspapers report on our schools; therefore, school administrations should have control over what is being published.

Write your own assertion.

Write your own assertion.

What's Your Opinion? © Prufrock Press Inc.

REASONING (PRO)

Petting and interacting with animals lowers anxiety and promotes positive thinking.	Hunting serves many purposes, including thinning overpopulated animal species and feeding needy families.
Athletics are very worthwhile extracurricular activities; however, academics must remain the focus of a student's work.	America prides itself on its Bill of Rights, which includes the freedom of speech. Can we grant our school newspapers anything less?
Write your own reasoning.	Write your own reasoning.

REASONING (CON)

There is a great deal of work associated with caring for pets (e.g., feeding them, walking them, cleaning up after them).

There is no sport in tracking down animals with motorized vehicles and shooting them with long-range weapons.

Many student athletes depend on athletic achievements to get a scholarship to college. They should not be banned from playing a sport because of a drop in grades.

Middle school and high school students are learning the responsibilities associated with the printed word. They need direction from adults.

Write your own reasoning.

Write your own reasoning.

What's Your Opinion? © Prufrock Press Inc.

EVIDENCE (PRO)

Studies have shown that interacting with cats and dogs lowers blood pressure more effectively than blood pressure medicine does.	A hunter's bullet is far more humane than slow starvation. Thousands of deer starved to death in the winter of 2007 due to harsh conditions. One moose can supply 500 lbs. of meat!
Colleges require athletes to maintain a minimum grade point average. If high schools do not provide their athletes with strong academic backgrounds, then athletic scholarships will not help athletes finish college.	Historically, censorship has led to an uninformed public. This is very dangerous in a democracy. The school newspaper is one of the few outlets students have to express their views and to inform fellow students.
Find and write your own evidence.	Find and write your own evidence.

EVIDENCE (CON)

The cost of owning a dog over an average lifetime (14 years) can range from $4,000–$40,000!

Hunters kill more than 130 million animals in the United States every year. This is a wasteful use of our natural animal resources.

Studies have shown that on average, student athletes perform better than nonathletes in the classroom. If athletes have a minimum grade requirement, then all students who participate in an activity should also have such a requirement.

School administrators have the responsibility to oversee published material to be certain that articles reflect the truth and do not exploit individuals. Parents have sued schools after their children were embarrassed in school newspapers.

Find and write your own evidence.

Find and write your own evidence.

CONLUSION (PRO)

Pet owners are healthier than those who do not own pets due to their interactions with their cats and dogs.

Hunting wild animals is a right that all Americans should continue to enjoy.

Student athletes must maintain a minimum G.P.A. in order to ensure that their academics do not suffer from their focus on athletics.

Freedom of speech is an American right guaranteed by the Constitution. Being a student should not result in being denied that right.

Write your own conclusion.

Write your own conclusion.

CONCLUSION (CON)

The cost of owning a pet is so high that it greatly increases the level of stress for pet owners.

Hunting is an unethical and cruel activity that is disguised as a sport.

Minimum G.P.A. requirements for student athletes are unfair and only serve to promote a negative stereotype.

Administrators should approve school newspapers before they go to press. It is the school's job to model responsible behavior.

Write your own conclusion.

Write your own conclusion.

What's Your Opinion? © Prufrock Press Inc.

Lesson 4

Concepts

- Assertions/opposing assertions
- Reasoning
- Evidence
- Conclusions

Materials

- Statements sheet (p. 62)
- Pattern of Refutation sheet (p. 63)
- Argument cards (pp. 51–58)
- Ball (such as a beach ball) or beanbag

Student Objective

The student demonstrates an understanding of refutation of an argument by participating in an improvisation game.

Introduction

Review with the students the concepts and argument parts covered in Lesson 3, including the opponents' assertion ("They say . . . "); an opposing assertion ("But we say . . . "); reasoning and evidence ("Because . . . "); and conclusion ("Therefore . . . ").

Recognition

Students should give verbal examples of each step. If you like, have them review their examples from Lesson 3.

Application

Students practice the steps by playing an improvisation and memory game. Be sure that the Pattern of Refutation sheet is available for students to look at as they play this game.

1. Students are divided into four teams (we recommend that you assign teams). Each team stands in one corner of the room.
2. You should stand in the center of the room, holding a small ball or beanbag. Using an assertion from the list provided (or an assertion of your choice), make a statement and toss the ball to one of the teams.
3. The receiving team must repeat the assertion, provide an opposing assertion, and toss the ball to the second team.
4. The second team begins by repeating the assertion and the opposition, and then fills in the reasoning.
5. The second team tosses the ball to the third team, which must repeat the entire sequence (assertion, opposition, and reasoning) and then provide evidence to support the argument. (This evidence can be made up.)
6. The third team then tosses the ball to the final team. This team must restate the assertion, opposition, reasoning, and evidence, and then state a conclusion.

Have the students play for several rounds.

Problem Solving

Have students develop their sense of the rhythm of refutation by staging arguments in front of the class.

1. Put students into groups. (You can keep the same groups you used for the ball toss, or you can put them into groups randomly or by interest.)
2. Students should brainstorm topics that are important to them and use the four steps of refutation to develop their arguments.
3. Groups of pro and con students should role-play their arguments in front of the class.

Grade-Level Expectations

The student:

- Recognizes organizational structures within paragraphs or texts (e.g., proposition, support).
- Exhibits logical organization and uses language appropriate for audience, context, and purpose.
- Includes smooth transitions, supports thesis with well-chosen details, and provides a coherent conclusion.

- Uses a variety of strategies of address (e.g., eye contact, speaking rate, volume, articulation, inflection, intonation, rhythm, gesture).
- Selects appropriate words or explains the use of words in context, including content-specific vocabulary, words with multiple meanings, or precise vocabulary.

Additional Notes

- It is essential that the students have a visual reference to use as they play this game. Either copy the pattern of refutation onto the blackboard, or post the provided sheet on an overhead or LCD screen.
- To help students grasp the concepts, first allow them to use the argument cards from Lesson 3 in order to practice the pattern of refutation. Once they have remembered the rhythm of the argument, they can move on to crafting original arguments.
- You will need space to play this game. It can be played successfully in a classroom, but desks will need to be moved to allow students to move freely enough.
- Choose your ball or other object carefully, keeping in mind safety and space. It is possible to use a small stuffed animal, so long as it is reasonably aerodynamic!
- Many students, experiencing debate for the first time, are finally able to put all of the concepts together during this game.

STATEMENTS

Backpacks should be banned from schools.	Students should be allowed to drop out of school after the eighth grade.
Report cards should be abolished.	Students should attend school year-round.
Schools should not be run by the government.	School uniforms should be required.
The school day should run until 4 p.m., but with no homework allowed.	Every student in the United States should be given a laptop computer to use in school.
The Internet should be free.	The driving age should be lowered to 14.
There should be more performing arts programs in schools.	Daylight Savings Time should be abandoned.
Every United States citizen should be required to register his or her fingerprints and DNA.	There should be laws limiting the size of private-use cars.
All United States citizens should be required to recycle.	School dances should allow students to bring guests from other schools.
All grades should be pass/fail.	If you were stranded on a desert island, it would be better to be there with your worst enemy than to be there alone.

What's Your Opinion? © Prufrock Press Inc.

PATTERN OF REFUTATION

THE TEACHER:
* makes an **assertion** ("They say . . . ").

TEAM 1:
* repeats the teacher's assertion ("They say . . . ") and
* adds an **opposing assertion** ("But we say . . . ").

TEAM 2:
* repeats the teacher's assertion ("They say . . . ");
* repeats Team 1's opposing assertion ("But we say . . . "); and
* adds **reasoning** ("Because . . . ").

TEAM 3:
* repeats the teacher's assertion ("They say . . . ");
* repeats Team 1's opposing assertion ("But we say . . . ");
* repeats Team 2's reasoning ("Because . . . "); and
* adds **evidence** ("We know this because . . . ").

TEAM 4:
* repeats the teacher's assertion ("They say . . . ");
* repeats Team 1's opposing assertion ("But we say . . . ");
* repeats Team 2's reasoning ("Because . . . ");
* repeats Team 3's evidence ("We know this because . . . "); and
* adds a **conclusion** ("Therefore . . . ").

Lesson 5

Concepts

- Using evidence to support reasoning
- Examples
- Analogy
- Cause and effect
- Costs vs. benefits

Materials

- Types of reasoning posters (pp. 67–70)
- Deduce the Reasoning sheet (p. 71)
- Reasoning cards (pp. 72–75)

Student Objective

The student demonstrates his or her ability to be persuasive by defending the choices made on a completed Deduce the Reasoning sheet.

Introduction

Begin a discussion of the four types of reasoning illustrated in this lesson. The four visual aids (posters) depicting the four types of reasoning should be posted around the room.

- Using an **example** means using an illustration of the debate issue to show how it has been resolved in the past. For example, "When I was failing my science class, the teacher let me do extra credit, and I pulled my grade up. Therefore, I would benefit from doing extra credit in English as well."
- Using **cause and effect** involves considering an instance of why something happens and what the result is once it has happened. For example, "When I

walk my dog every day, he is much calmer for the rest of the day. Therefore, dog owners should walk their dogs at least once a day so they are calm."

- Weighing **costs vs. benefits** means evaluating an action according to whether it would cause more harm than good or vice versa. For example, "Walking my dog every day has increased his health, and my vet bills are much lower than they used to be. Although his daily walk takes up an hour of my time, it is well worth it. Therefore, people should go on long walks with their dogs."
- Drawing an **analogy** means making a comparison between people, places, events, or ideas. For example, "Kids say that homework is a waste of time, but no one would expect an athlete to improve his or her skills without practicing. Therefore, homework should be used as a way to practice school skills."

Recognition

Students demonstrate understanding by explaining the concepts verbally and through their discussion examples.

Application

Distribute the Deduce the Reasoning sheet to students. Using the following method, they should find and analyze one example of each type of reasoning.
1.   Choose a reasoning card.
2.   Read the card and choose the type of reasoning it demonstrates.
3.   Analyze the reasoning according to the sheet instructions.
4.   Replace the reasoning card.
5.   Choose another card.

Problem Solving

Students can defend their choices in several ways:
1.   Write a short report defending their choices.
2.   Present these reports.
3.   Discuss the activity without doing a written report.

You can offer feedback or collect and grade student work at your discretion.

Grade-Level Expectations

The student:
- Selects and summarizes key ideas from a set context.
- Connects what has been read to prior knowledge and to other texts by referring to and explaining relevant ideas.
- States and maintains a focus, a firm judgment, or a point of view when responding to a given question.

- Uses specific details, refers to texts, or cites relevant material to support focus or judgment.
- Organizes ideas, uses transitional words/phrases, and writes a conclusion that provides closure.
- Selects appropriate words or explains the use of words in context, including content-specific vocabulary, words with multiple meanings, or precise vocabulary.
- Evaluates information presented in terms of relevance.
- Uses evidence to support conclusions.

Additional Notes

- Reasoning cards can fit into more than one category, representing multiple types of reasoning. Students should be able to justify their answers. The process of thinking through their rationales will reinforce learning!
- Some of the students will need to be encouraged to share their reasoning and rationales. Be sure to emphasize that there is not necessarily one correct answer.

EXAMPLES

Examples are used to illustrate when the issue being debated has occurred and what the result has been in that situation.

HISTORICAL
An example that was true in the past

CONTEMPORARY
An example that is currently true

HYPOTHETICAL
An example that might be true in the future

CAUSE AND EFFECT

Causal reasoning focuses on why something happened in order to give evidence for or against an assertion.

GUIDELINES FOR CAUSAL REASONING

- Everything that happens or exists has a cause.

- A cause is not the same as a coincidence.

- Determining a cause is often difficult.

- Events can have both immediate and long-term effects.

- Effects are often observed long after the cause has occurred.

- The effect often depends on the response to a cause.

COST VERSUS BENEFITS

This involves evaluating an action by whether it causes more harm than good or vice versa.

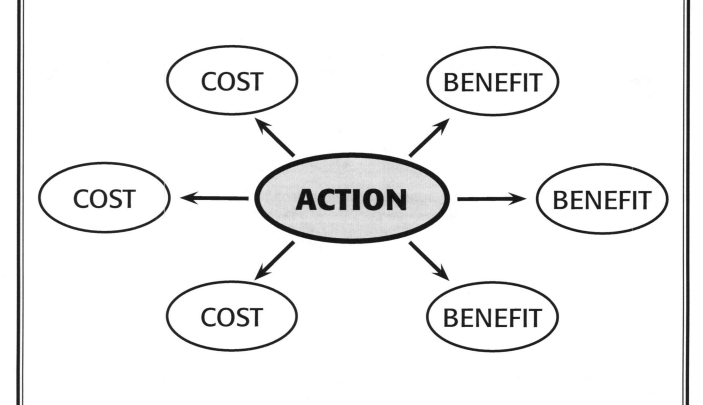

ANALOGY

An analogy is a comparison made between people, places, events, or ideas to support an argument.

HOW STRONG IS THE ANALOGY?

DO THE SIMILARITIES OUTWEIGH THE DIFFERENCES?

DEDUCE THE REASONING

REASONING STATEMENTS
A. _____
_____
B. _____
_____
C. _____
_____
D. _____
_____

EXAMPLE	ANALOGY	CAUSE AND EFFECT	COSTS VS. BENEFITS
Does this reasoning give an illustration of when the debate issue has been true and what the result was in that situation?	Does this reasoning make a comparison between people, places, events, or ideas?	Does this reasoning focus on why something happened and what the result was in that situation?	Does this reasoning evaluate an action by whether it causes more harm than good or vice versa?
↓	↓	↓	↓
When did the example happen? Does the example relate directly to the topic? Is the example hypothetical? Does this example offer pro or con reasoning?	What is being compared in this analogy? What are the similarities between the compared people, places, events, or ideas? What are the differences? Does this analogy offer pro or con reasoning?	What is the cause part of this reasoning? What is the effect part? Is it a coincidence, which is not causal? Does this use of cause and effect offer pro or con reasoning?	What is the action? What are the costs of making this action? What are the benefits? Does this weighing of costs vs. benefits offer pro or con reasoning?

What's Your Opinion? © Prufrock Press Inc.   71

Permission is granted to photocopy or reproduce this page for single classroom use only.

Name:_____ Date: _____

REASONING CARDS

When the middle schools tried to require students to wear uniforms last year, the parents were furious!	National studies on schools that require school uniforms have found that these schools' students have higher test scores.
New students at schools that require school uniforms report that they feel accepted much sooner than students in schools without uniform requirements.	Student fundraisers that include homemade baked goods report higher sales than those that don't include these items.
Discipline referrals increased when students were allowed to buy sugary treats during lunch.	Teachers report more afternoon headaches when students eat sugary treats during lunch.

REASONING CARDS

Catholic school students wear uniforms to school. They also score higher on the New England Common Assessments Program (NECAP) tests than public school students do. If public schools required uniforms, their students would have higher NECAP scores.

Although the cost of a school uniform is higher than the average cost of a school outfit, students do not need to buy so many clothes overall, as they can just rewear their uniforms. So in the end, wearing uniforms cuts down on families' clothing costs.

In schools that require uniforms, students are less creative in art classes than they are in schools that do not require uniforms.

When we have a bake sale, we raise about $100. When we sell popcorn, we only make $50.

Students who eat chocolate at lunch have a shorter attention span than students who do not eat chocolate at lunch.

School cafeterias are not allowed to sell sweets, because sweets are not healthy for students. Should student groups be allowed to sell them?

What's Your Opinion? © Prufrock Press Inc.

Permission is granted to photocopy or reproduce this page for single classroom use only.

73

REASONING CARDS

In the 1950s, most school had policies requiring uniforms, and it was found that uniforms severely stunted students' individuality.	If we had school uniforms in our district, then as new students came into our schools, they would immediately feel as though they belonged, because they would look like everyone else.
In my old school, uniforms were required. Boys wore coats and ties, and girls had to wear skirts. This was completely unfair during the winter when it was very cold.	Once we had a bake sale at school, and teachers complained that the kids were "off the wall" afterward, during their afternoon classes.
Last year our theater group held two bake sales to raise money for the show. They were very successful—we raised more than $200!	If the student council had a bake sale, everyone would contribute delicious baked goods to raise money for the dance.

REASONING CARDS

Bake sales raise more money for schools, but they adversely affect students' attention spans on the day of the sale.

Having a bake sale is a lucrative way to raise money for school events, but it requires parents and students to spend time and money baking the goods.

Students wholeheartedly support bake sales in schools. They enjoy baking the goods to be sold. However, teachers report a decrease in students' attention spans the day of the sale.

School uniforms ensure an appropriate dress code among students, but the initial cost of the uniforms can be a burden on families.

Studies have shown that school uniforms are strongly associated with an increase in test scores, but students report greatly disliking them.

The use of school uniforms produces fewer discipline issues, higher grades, and stronger school spirit. However, uniforms are associated with a drop in creativity.

Lesson 6

Concepts

- Being a stakeholder
- Point of view

Materials

- Teacher key/organizers for topics and characters (pp. 79–81)
- Character profiles with and without corresponding reasoning (pp. 82–117)

Student Objective

The student demonstrates an understanding of the concept of "stakeholder" by role-playing a given point of view in an argument.

Introduction

Demonstrate the concept of what a stakeholder is by using an argument topic that is certain to provoke discussion (e.g., "Boys' sports teams deserve more field time, because they have more games"). Then, ask for comments and allow students to debate, prompting them to express their personal feelings. Stop the discussion midstream and identify the stakeholders in the debate. (For the given example, a football player may have been on the pro side, while a girls' field hockey player may have been on the con side.) Discuss the concept of being a stakeholder—that is, having a vested interest in the outcome of an argument.

Recognition

Students participate in a discussion centered on why stakeholders have strong opinions.

Application

This lesson begins the final segment of the unit, in which students are introduced to the characters they will play during the authentic performance assessment (the final debate).

1. Students read their characters' profiles or, if you are allowing them to create their own characters, invent character profiles.
2. Students brainstorm lists of reasons that their characters hold their respective points of view.
3. Remind students that their roles do not necessarily represent their own views!

Problem Solving

Students work in teams to begin preparing for the final debate.

1. Group students according to topics. We have provided three topics, but you should feel free to craft your own if you wish. We recommend that you assign all three topics so that students do not get bored, but if you prefer, you can have all students debating on the same topic. So long as there is an even number of teams (and each team has an opposing team on its same topic), then any combination is fine.
2. Assign teams to pro and con sides of their topics, and distribute character profiles (see Additional Notes section). If students complain, remind them that they are not necessarily representing their own viewpoints.
3. If you decide that students need guidance before researching their topics, you may want to create research source sheets for them. On these sheets, you can provide useful websites, background information, and search tips.
4. Each team then brainstorms a list of possible sources from which evidence will be gathered. Students will need to support their assigned characters' assertions.

Grade-Level Expectations

The student:
*   Selects and summarizes key ideas for the given context.
*   Connects what has been read to prior knowledge and to other texts by referring to and explaining relevant ideas.
*   States and maintains a focus, a firm judgment, or a point of view when responding to a given question.
*   Exhibits logical organization and uses language appropriate for audience, context, and purpose.
*   Identifies potential sources of information.

Additional Notes

- The stakeholder discussion introduces the concept of point of view; the discussion can also be used to reinforce students' existing concepts of point of view that they have learned from language arts class. Thus, you might have a discussion about point of view wherein you connect debate to novels or texts you've had students read. Although this is effective, it is not necessary to the implementation of the unit overall.

- Topic sheets are included in the materials following this lesson for teacher reference. We recommend that you find websites to use in a discussion of how to research topics. Depending on how much background students have in using the Internet for research, you might provide them with URLs of sites to explore, or you might elect to show the class examples before they begin, discussing what makes Internet sources reliable. Lesson 8 involves further discussion of research options.

- We have included two types of stakeholder cards. The first type includes not only each character's pro or con assertion, but also an explanation of why the character feels the way he or she does about the assigned topic. The second type of stakeholder card includes only the pro or con assertion, allowing students more flexibility regarding their research and lines of reasoning. You can choose to give all of your students the same type of card, students can choose whether they want cards with reasons included, or you can determine which students should get which cards based on their strengths and weaknesses. (Or, as a final option, you can select topics and have students make up their own characters.)

- When choosing which of these options is best for your students, it is important that you reflect on what you want them to focus on. If you decide to emphasize defending strong viewpoints through debate, you will want to use the provided viewpoints, necessitating that students focus on research and logical support. If you want your students to develop their own points of view and defend them, you may want to give them more freedom in terms of researching, reasoning, and developing opposing arguments, thereby building their critical thinking skills. If you have a group that is struggling with the structure and nature of debate, you will probably elect to use the provided viewpoints as stepping stones. We have provided a template for blank cards that you can fill in or have students fill in, should you choose to give them a lot of freedom regarding characters and reasoning. It is really up to you how and whether to use the provided cards.

TOPIC 1

Should students be allowed to carry/use cell phones and other electronic devices in schools?

Stakeholders	Pro	Con
Students	Art student	Honor student
	Newspaper editor	Basketball player
Teachers	Technology teacher	Art teacher
	Football coach	Social studies teacher
Parents	Stockbroker	President of the PTO
Administrators	School secretary	Assistant principal

What's Your Opinion? © Prufrock Press Inc.

Permission is granted to photocopy or reproduce this page for single classroom use only.

79

TOPIC 2

Should the school require a dress code and/or uniforms?

Stakeholders	Pro	Con
Students	Cheerleader	Honor student
	New student	Music student
Teachers	Science teacher	Guidance counselor
	Physical education teacher	Math teacher
Parents	Shop owner	Therapist
Administrators	Superintendent	School psychologist

TOPIC 3

Should schools have the right to search student lockers? Should students and staff be required to pass through metal detectors?

Stakeholders	Pro	Con
Students	Soccer player	Captain of the debate team
	Honor student	New student
Teachers	Band director	English teacher
	Security officer	Family and consumer science teacher
Parents	Stay-at-home mom	Newspaper editor
Administrators	Principal	School district lawyer

TOPIC 1: Pro

Student (Newspaper Editor)
Yes, students should be allowed to carry and/or use cell phones and other electronic devices on school property. As the editor of the school newspaper, I feel strongly about our constitutional rights and freedoms. It seems to me that restricting our use of communication tools is a direct attack on our personal freedoms! Cell phones have become an integral part of our modern lives, and they can no longer be ignored in the academic world.

Student (Newspaper Editor)
Yes, students should be allowed to carry and/or use cell phones and other electronic devices on school property.

Teacher (Football Coach)

Yes, students should be allowed to carry and/ or use cell phones and other electronic devices on school property. Cell phones have been the best addition to our "equipment" in the last 10 years! Coaches use them to communicate across the field. Also, the use of cell phones has cut down considerably on the number of hours that we spend waiting with students whose parents have forgotten to pick them up from practice.

Teacher (Football Coach)

Yes, students should be allowed to carry and/or use cell phones and other electronic devices on school property.

Teacher (Technology Expert)

Yes, students should be allowed to carry and/or use cell phones and other electronic devices on school property. It is our goal, as members of the technology department, to equip our students to function successfully in our technological age. We should not prohibit them from using the most basic of technological tools.

Teacher (Technology Expert)

Yes, students should be allowed to carry and/or use cell phones and other electronic devices on school property.

Parent (Stockbroker)

Yes, students should be allowed to carry and/or use cell phones and other electronic devices on school property. All students should be allowed to carry their cell phones so that parents can contact them in case of emergency. Likewise, students should be allowed to contact their parents at appropriate times throughout the school day when they need parental assistance.

Parent (Stockbroker)

Yes, students should be allowed to carry and/or use cell phones and other electronic devices on school property.

Administrator (School Secretary)

Yes, students should be allowed to carry and/or use cell phones and other electronic devices on school property. It is a terrible inconvenience when students constantly come into the office to call home. It would solve a great many logistical problems if students had access to their own phones. Middle school students are old enough to handle the responsibility of having phones with them.

Administrator (School Secretary)

Yes, students should be allowed to carry and/or use cell phones and other electronic devices on school property.

What's Your Opinion? © Prufrock Press Inc.
Permission is granted to photocopy or reproduce this page for single classroom use only.

Student (Artist)

Yes, students should be allowed to carry and/or use cell phones and other electronic devices on school property. I feel strongly that it is a matter of personal liberty that we be allowed the use of cell phones. Having said that, students should act responsibly with their phones and be respectful of others. After all, school is where we need to learn to act responsibly. This is an opportunity to practice responsibility.

Student (Artist)

Yes, students should be allowed to carry and/or use cell phones and other electronic devices on school property.

TOPIC 1: Con

Student (Honor Student)
No, students should not be allowed to carry and/or use cell phones and other electronic devices on school property. Cell phones are the new tools for bullying in schools. Students use text messaging to send nasty comments to other students during the school day. It is cruel, and schools need to protect students from this new form of social torture.

Student (Honor Student)
No, students should not be allowed to carry and/or use cell phones and other electronic devices on school property.

Parent (President of the PTO)

No, students should not be allowed to carry and/or use cell phones and other electronic devices on school property. Our students are bombarded by distractions from the outside world at every waking moment. The Internet, instant messaging, cell phones, and e-mail provide a barrage of information and communication at every hour of every day. The school is in a position to protect our students and allow them a safe haven from the overload of information. The school cannot shirk this responsibility.

Parent (President of the PTO)

No, students should not be allowed to carry and/or use cell phones and other electronic devices on school property.

What's Your Opinion? © Prufrock Press Inc.

Permission is granted to photocopy or reproduce this page for single classroom use only.

89

Student (Basketball Player)

No, students should not be allowed to carry and/or use cell phones and other electronic devices on school property. I find cell phones very distracting during classes. A couple of weeks ago, I was taking an algebra test, and somebody's phone started ringing. I had almost figured out how to solve a problem, and the ringtone completely broke my train of thought. It is bad enough that the office buzzes people in the classrooms. We don't need any more auditory distractions when we're trying to concentrate. I'm having a hard enough time maintaining athletic eligibility—I don't need another distraction.

Student (Basketball Player)

No, students should not be allowed to carry and/or use cell phones and other electronic devices on school property.

Teacher (Art Teacher)

No, students should not be allowed to carry and/ or use cell phones and other electronic devices on school property. Every time a cell phone rings in my classroom, it completely disrupts the focus we have achieved. I understand the need for parents to be able to reach their children after school, but I see no reason that students need to have access to their phones during school hours.

Teacher (Art Teacher)

No, students should not be allowed to carry and/or use cell phones and other electronic devices on school property.

Teacher (Social Studies Teacher)
No, students should not be allowed to carry and/or use cell phones and other electronic devices on school property. My students are much too distracted by social interaction. It is the nature of middle school students. We must provide an "island of calm" for students by restricting cell phone use. It is our responsibility as the adults in their lives to provide them with limits.

Teacher (Social Studies Teacher)
No, students should not be allowed to carry and/or use cell phones and other electronic devices on school property.

Administrator (Assistant Principal)

No, students should not be allowed to carry and/or use cell phones and other electronic devices on school property. I spend a considerable amount of time every day confiscating cell phones from students who are using them during the school day. Cell phones are a terrible distraction to the education process. Our students do not have the maturity to use their cell phones responsibly, so we must make the decision for them!

Administrator (Assistant Principle)

No, students should not be allowed to carry and/or use cell phones and other electronic devices on school property.

Create your own characters and points of view with these cards.

What's Your Opinion? © Prufrock Press Inc.

TOPIC 2: Pro

Student (Cheerleader)
Yes, the school should require a dress code and/or a uniform. On game days, we wear our cheerleading uniforms to school. I have noticed that on these days, I am much more focused on schoolwork. Although I like to choose my own clothes, I think that having uniforms or following a dress code would help many students to be more successful in school.

Student (Cheerleader)
Yes, the school should require a dress code and/or a uniform.

Student (New Student)

Yes, the school should require a dress code and/ or a uniform. I have only been a student here for a month. I entered the school in the middle of the year. It is very difficult to fit in, because I moved here from a different part of the country. All of the clothes that I like to wear make me stand out as different in this new school. It would be so much easier if there were a uniform. That way, I would have looked like I belonged from the first day.

Student (New Student)

Yes, the school should require a dress code and/or a uniform.

Teacher (Physical Education Teacher)

Yes, the school should require a dress code and/or a uniform. In my classes, I can see a marked difference in my students when they are wearing their gym uniforms. I am absolutely convinced that if they were to wear uniforms to all of their classes, their academics would improve.

Teacher (Physical Education Teacher)

Yes, the school should require a dress code and/or a uniform.

Teacher (Science Teacher)

Yes, the school should require a dress code and/ or a uniform. As I watch students arrive for school each morning, I am amazed at the clothing they choose to wear. It is an area in which students continually opt to push the envelope in the name of individuality. Having a strong dress code or a uniform policy would help teachers; that way, we wouldn't have to navigate this "how to dress" battlefield.

Teacher (Science Teacher)

Yes, the school should require a dress code and/or a uniform.

Parent (Shop Owner)

Yes, the school should require a dress code and/ or a uniform. That would make it much more cost-efficient for me to buy uniforms for my child. It would also eliminate the issue of students wearing inappropriate clothing to school. I try to monitor my child, but I can't pay close attention all of the time.

Parent (Shop Owner)

Yes, the school should require a dress code and/or a uniform.

Administrator (District Superintendent)

Yes, the school should require a dress code and/or a uniform. Our students would have a better image of themselves and of the role that school plays in their lives if they wore uniforms. Uniforms would eliminate many behavioral issues and help students to focus on the business of learning, not impressing their peers.

Administrator (District Superintendent)

Yes, the school should require a dress code and/or a uniform.

TOPIC 2: Con

Teacher (Guidance Counselor)
No, the school should not require a dress code and/or a uniform. The last thing that our students need is more rules. They spend far too much time fighting against the rules that we already have in place. It is imperative for them to have some kind of control over their own lives.

Teacher (Guidance Counselor)
No, the school should not require a dress code and/or a uniform.

Student (Honor Student)

No, the school should not require a dress code and/or a uniform. Many people think that if the school can make all of us look alike, then we will get better grades. Well, I have a very individual fashion style, and I have been an honor student for 3 years. Making somebody dress a certain way is only a way to control what he or she looks like—it can't control the way someone thinks!

Student (Honor Student)

No, the school should not require a dress code and/or a uniform.

Teacher (Math Teacher)
No, the school should not require a dress code and/or a uniform. I have been teaching in a middle school for the last 20 years. There are many things that I require of my students. I have far too many battles to fight as it is—the last thing I need is another area in which my students can test my limits.

Teacher (Math Teacher)
No, the school should not require a dress code and/or a uniform.

Student (Music Student)
No, the school should not require a dress code and/or a uniform. As students, we are required to follow many rules, and we are given very little choice. I do not see why we should have our choice of clothing taken away.

Student (Music Student)
No, the school should not require a dress code and/or a uniform.

Administrator (School Psychologist)
No, the school should not require a dress code and/ or a uniform. Restricting our students' right to choose something as individual as clothing is in direct conflict with our goal of teaching students to make good choices. If they do not get the chance to make choices, then they'll never learn to make good ones.

Administrator (School Psychologist)
No, the school should not require a dress code and/or a uniform.

Parent (Therapist)
No, the school should not require a dress code
and/or a uniform. It is especially important
that students in middle school be encouraged
to express their individuality. It will crush
their emerging independence if they are told
what they must wear to school every day.

Parent (Therapist)
No, the school should not require a
dress code and/or a uniform.

TOPIC 3: Pro

Student (Soccer Player)

Yes, schools should have the right to search students' lockers and should require students and staff to pass through metal detectors. Kids shouldn't bring weapons, drugs, or other contraband materials to school. If students knew that the principal could search their lockers at any time, then they would think twice about bringing in any of these items. I think that the school has the responsibility to do everything it can to keep us safe.

Student (Soccer Player)

Yes, schools should have the right to search students' lockers and should require students and staff to pass through metal detectors.

What's Your Opinion? © Prufrock Press Inc.

Permission is granted to photocopy or reproduce this page for single classroom use only.

107

Staff (Security Officer)

Yes, schools should have the right to search students' lockers and should require students and staff to pass through metal detectors. If I have to get a warrant to search a student's locker, it will just slow down our whole system. It is my job to enforce the rules of the school and the laws of our country. The lockers are school property, so the school has the right to open and search them at any time.

Staff (Security Officer)

Yes, schools should have the right to search students' lockers and should require students and staff to pass through metal detectors.

Administrator (Principal)

Yes, schools should have the right to search students' lockers and should require students and staff to pass through metal detectors. If someone has nothing to hide, then why would it be an issue of personal freedoms? The bottom line is that I have to keep students safe from the moment they walk in until the moment they leave. The safety of everyone is the most important issue.

Administrator (Principal)

Yes, schools should have the right to search students' lockers and should require students and staff to pass through metal detectors.

Teacher (Band Director)

Yes, schools should have the right to search students' lockers and should require students and staff to pass through metal detectors. Students should not have the right to hide items in their lockers knowing that authorities cannot search there. It is already difficult enough for schools to keep students under control. We need the right to search.

Teacher (Band Director)

Yes, schools should have the right to search students' lockers and should require students and staff to pass through metal detectors.

What's Your Opinion? © Prufrock Press Inc.

Student (Honor Student)

Yes, schools should have the right to search students' lockers and should require students and staff to pass through metal detectors. I do not understand what the big deal is about this issue. I don't care if someone wants to look in my locker. I don't have anything to hide. I would rather feel safe while I am at school.

Student (Honor Student)

Yes, schools should have the right to search students' lockers and should require students and staff to pass through metal detectors.

Parent (Stay-At-Home Mother)
Yes, schools should have the right to search students' lockers and should require students and staff to pass through metal detectors. I want to have the peace of mind of knowing that the schools are doing everything they can to protect my children.

Parent (Stay-At-Home Mother)
Yes, schools should have the right to search students' lockers and should require students and staff to pass through metal detectors.

What's Your Opinion? © Prufrock Press Inc.

TOPIC 3: Con

Student (Captain of the Debate Team)
No, schools should not have the right to search students' lockers and should not require students and staff to pass through metal detectors. Students are citizens of the United States. The fact that we are minors does not matter when it comes to personal rights.

Student (Captain of the Debate Team)
No, schools should not have the right to search students' lockers and should not require students and staff to pass through metal detectors.

Administrator (School District Lawyer)

No, schools should not have the right to search students' lockers and should not require students and staff to pass through metal detectors. This is a very complicated area of the law. Searching lockers and requiring metal detectors in every school will have us tied up in court for the next 20 years. I do not believe that such measures would be worth the small measure of comfort that they would afford the community.

Administrator (School District Lawyer)

No, schools should not have the right to search students' lockers and should not require students and staff to pass through metal detectors.

What's Your Opinion? © Prufrock Press Inc.

Teacher (Family and Consumer Science)

No, schools should not have the right to search students' lockers and should not require students and staff to pass through metal detectors. We work very hard to communicate a sense of trust and respect to our students. We will ruin that trust by requiring them to submit to random searches and enter school through a metal detector.

Teacher (Family and Consumer Science)

No, schools should not have the right to search students' lockers and should not require students and staff to pass through metal detectors.

Student (New Student)

No, schools should not have the right to search students' lockers and should not require students and staff to pass through metal detectors. In my last school, the administration installed a metal detector. After 6 months, student morale was so low that the metal detector was removed. Safety had increased, but the school's sense of community had been destroyed.

Student (New Student)

No, schools should not have the right to search students' lockers and should not require students and staff to pass through metal detectors.

Parent (Newspaper Editor)

No, schools should not have the right to search students' lockers and should not require students and staff to pass through metal detectors. We live in the United States of America, where personal property rights are guaranteed by the Constitution.

Parent (Newspaper Editor)

No, schools should not have the right to search students' lockers and should not require students and staff to pass through metal detectors.

Lesson 7

Concepts

- Making and opposing assertions
- Using reasoning and evidence
- Drawing conclusions

Materials

- Topic prompts (pp. 121–123)
- Final debate rubrics (pp. 124–125)
- Argument Outline sheets (pp. 126–127)
- Argument cards (pp. 128–134)

Student Objective

The student demonstrates an understanding of the parts of an argument by using the Argument Outline sheets to prepare for the debate.

Introduction

Hand out the prompt and rubric for the authentic performance assessment (final debate). Either read the prompt and rubric aloud, or have students read them aloud.

Recognition

Students give examples of the type of work discussed in the rubrics that will be used to score the final debates.

Application

Using the following steps, students organize their teams.

1. Students introduce themselves as their characters and state their beliefs on the debate topic.
2. Students work in teams to fill in the first part of the Argument Outline sheet.
3. Students brainstorm reasoning that each character might use to present his or her point of view.
4. Students make a list of possible Internet sites or reference books that may provide evidence for the reasoning they have chosen.
5. Students have the teacher sign off on their Argument Outline sheets, allowing them to proceed to the computer room to begin the research phase.

Problem Solving

Students put their knowledge of refutation and opposition into practice.

1. Members of each team put themselves in the opposing team members' shoes by making a list of possible reasoning and evidence that the opposing side of the debate might use.
2. Students then take steps to organize their own evidence, using the provided materials, in preparation for counteracting their opponents' arguments.

Grade-Level Expectations

The student:

- Connects what has been read to prior knowledge and to other texts by referring to and explaining relevant ideas.
- Uses specific details, references to text, or relevant citations to support a focus or judgment.
- Identifies potential sources of information and evaluates the relevance of presented information.
- Gathers, organizes, analyzes, and interprets information and uses evidence to support conclusions.
- Selects appropriate words or explains the use of words in context, including content-specific vocabulary, words with multiple meanings, and precise vocabulary.
- Uses information from the text to answer questions, to state the main ideas, and to provide supporting details.
- Draws inferences about a text, including the author's purpose or message.
- Uses evidence to form or evaluate opinions, judgments, or assertions about the relevant central ideas.
- Distinguishes fact from opinion and identifies possible bias, propaganda, or conflicting information within or across texts.
- Makes inferences about causes or effects.

- The first two prompts are on issues that are challenging but direct, asking students to argue on the topic of either uniforms or cell phones in schools. The third prompt covers both locker searches and metal detectors, making students' research and arguments more complex. For this reason, we have included a separate rubric for the third prompt. This way, you can discuss with students the importance of taking additional variables into account when researching, offering evidence, and considering the opposing side's argument.

- It should be noted, however, that because of the phrasing of the first two prompts, each of these could also be interpreted as having more than one simple topic. The differences between uniforms and a dress code, as well as those between cell phones and other electronic devices, could be emphasized if you wish to provide additional opportunities for differentiation to your students. If you choose to do this, you can adapt the rubric for the third prompt to fit the first and second prompts. Otherwise—if you believe these first two topics are too broad—you should tweak them (e.g., eliminate "dress code" or "other electronic devices" from the prompts). Use the prompt and rubric combination that works best for your class.

- For Prompt 3, students are encouraged to interview experts. If possible, provide them with contact information for lawyers or human rights experts.

Lesson 7

Name:_____ Date: _____

PROMPT 1

The middle schools in your area have had terrible publicity lately. Students, parents, teachers, and administrators have been disagreeing on appropriate behavior. Students have been complaining about proposed dress codes and locker searches. Teachers are concerned about the use of cell phones by students in the building, and several students have been suspended for having them. Everyone is concerned about weapons, and some are trying to get metal detectors put in each school. But questions remain in everyone's mind: Are these measures appropriate? Will these measures solve the problems?

You have been chosen by your principal as a representative to serve on a committee of middle school students, parents, teachers, and administrators to address the issues. Your job is to research the issue listed below and suggest a practical solution that will be acceptable to the majority of people involved. As you work to help establish new rules and guidelines for middle school students, your opinions should reflect the factual information you have gained from the research and from your character profile. Your issue is as follows:

SHOULD STUDENTS BE ALLOWED TO CARRY CELL PHONES AND OTHER ELECTRONIC DEVICES IN SCHOOL?

To prepare for the committee meeting of school representatives, you must do the following:

- Research the issue and the options involved in resolving it. (You will turn in your list of sources. Be sure to use the formatting and style that your teacher instructs you to use when citing sources so that it is clear where you found your information.)
- Formulate your opinion about the issue based on your research findings and character profile.
- Develop an argument expressing an opinion using the following criteria:
  - o **State your opinion.** Your opening statement should include a topic sentence clearly stating your opinion about the issue.
  - o **Support your opinion.** Each Argument Point card should give one reason for your opinion, along with supporting facts.
  - o **Summarize your position.** Your concluding statement should restate your opinion.

Remember that your argument should be designed to persuade the other members of the committee.

These prompts and rubrics were based on the work of Drs. Moon, Brighton, Callahan, and Tomlinson under the Educational Research and Development Centers PR/Award Number R206R50001. All rights permission secured.

Name:_____ Date: _____

PROMPT 2

The middle schools in your area have had terrible publicity lately. Students, parents, teachers, and administrators have been disagreeing on appropriate behavior. Students have been complaining about proposed dress codes and locker searches. Teachers are concerned about the use of cell phones by students in the building, and several students have been suspended for having them. Everyone is concerned about weapons, and some are trying to get metal detectors put in each school. But questions remain in everyone's mind: Are these measures appropriate? Will these measures solve the problems?

You have been chosen by your principal as a representative to serve on a committee of middle school students, parents, teachers, and administrators to address the issues. Your job is to research the issue listed below and suggest a practical solution that will be acceptable to the majority of people involved. As you work to help establish new rules and guidelines for middle school students, your opinions should reflect the factual information you have gained from the research and from your character profile. Your issue is as follows:

SHOULD THE SCHOOL REQUIRE A DRESS CODE AND/OR UNIFORMS?

To prepare for the committee meeting of school representatives, you must do the following:

- Research the issue and the options involved in resolving it. (You will turn in your list of sources. Be sure to use the formatting and style that your teacher instructs you to use when citing sources so that it is clear where you found your information.)
- Formulate your opinion about the issue based on your research findings and character profile.
- Develop an argument expressing an opinion using the following criteria:
   o **State your opinion.** Your opening statement should include a topic sentence clearly stating your opinion about the issue.
   o **Support your opinion.** Each Argument Point card should give one reason for your opinion, along with supporting facts.
   o **Summarize your position.** Your concluding statement should restate your opinion.

Remember that your argument should be designed to persuade the other members of the committee.

These prompts and rubrics were based on the work of Drs. Moon, Brighton, Callahan, and Tomlinson under the Educational Research and Development Centers PR/Award Number R206R50001. All rights permission secured.

What's Your Opinion? © Prufrock Press Inc.

Name:_____ Date: _____

PROMPT 3

The middle schools in your area have had terrible publicity lately. Students, parents, teachers, and administrators have been disagreeing on appropriate behavior. Students have been complaining about proposed dress codes and locker searches. Teachers are concerned about the use of cell phones by students in the building, and several students have been suspended for having them. Everyone is concerned about weapons, and some are trying to get metal detectors put in each school. But questions remain in everyone's mind: Are these measures appropriate? Will these measures solve the problems?

You have been chosen by your principal as a representative to serve on a committee of middle school students, parents, teachers, and administrators to address the issues. Your job is to research the issue listed below and suggest a practical solution that will be acceptable to the majority of people involved. As you work to help establish new rules and guidelines for middle school students, your opinions should reflect the factual information you have gained from the research and from your character profile. Your issue is as follows:

SHOULD SCHOOLS HAVE THE RIGHT TO SEARCH STUDENTS' LOCKERS? SHOULD STUDENTS AND STAFF BE REQUIRED TO PASS THROUGH METAL DETECTORS?

(*Note:* It may be helpful to interview a lawyer or other expert in the field of human rights to help formulate your opinion.)

To prepare for the committee meeting of school representatives, you must do the following:

* Research the issue and the options involved in resolving it. (You will turn in your list of sources. Be sure to use the formatting and style that your teacher instructs you to use when citing sources so that it is clear where you found your information.)
* Formulate your opinion about the issue based on your research findings and character profile.
* Develop an argument expressing an opinion using the following criteria:
  o **State your opinion.** Your opening statement should include a topic sentence clearly stating your opinion about the issue.
  o **Support your opinion.** Each Argument Point card should give one reason for your opinion, along with supporting facts.
  o **Summarize your position.** Your concluding statement should restate your opinion.

Remember that your argument should be designed to persuade the other members of the committee.

These prompts and rubrics were based on the work of Drs. Moon, Brighton, Callahan, and Tomlinson under the Educational Research and Development Centers PR/Award Number R206R50001. All rights permission secured.

RUBRIC FOR PROMPTS 1 & 2

	EXPERT	APPRENTICE	NOVICE
RESEARCH SOURCES	You provide complete background research sources. The committee gains a deep understanding of your side of the issue. Sources are cited in a professional formatting style.	You provide background research sources, but they do not cover all of your argument points. You cite sources, but you do not use a professional formatting style.	You do not provide background research sources, or your sources do not support your argument.
DEFENSE OF OPINIONS/ ABILITY TO PERSUADE	You state your opinions clearly and concisely. You use research to thoroughly support your opinions. The committee is convinced that your ideas are best.	You state and defend your opinions, but you do not make specific references to the research. The committee feels that they need more information before accepting your ideas.	You state your opinions, but you do not defend them. You have not given enough supporting information to make the committee believe that your opinions are valid.
SPEAKING STYLE	Your argument is appropriately tailored to your audience. You use effective vocabulary. Ideas flow smoothly from your introduction to your conclusion. The main idea is evident throughout the argument and is supported by rich detail.	In general, your argument is well tailored to your audience. You have a clear opening statement, argument points, and a conclusion centered on a main idea, although your transitions are choppy.	Your argument is not tailored to the committee's purpose; too many assumptions are made about what the committee knows. A single main idea is difficult to follow in the argument. Supporting details are not provided, making the argument's structure unclear.
PRESENTATION	You are clear and consistent in volume. Your body posture and delivery make it clear that you know your facts, lending credibility to your opinion.	You are believable in your role at times. However, it is sometimes hard to hear you, giving the impression that you are unsure of your opinion.	Your speech is difficult to hear due to volume and/or pace, and it is hard to believe your opinion due to lack of conviction.

These prompts and rubrics were based on the work of Drs. Moon, Brighton, Callahan, and Tomlinson under the Educational Research and Development Centers PR/Award Number R206R50001. All rights permission secured.

RUBRIC FOR PROMPT 3

	EXPERT	APPRENTICE	NOVICE
RESEARCH SOURCES	You provide complete background research sources. The committee gains a deep understanding of your side of the issue. Sources are cited in a professional formatting style.	You provide background research sources, but they do not cover all of your argument points. You cite sources, but you do not use a professional formatting style.	You do not provide background research sources, or your sources do not support your argument.
DEFENSE OF OPINIONS/ ABILITY TO PERSUADE	You state your opinions clearly and concisely. You use research to thoroughly support your opinions. The committee is convinced that your ideas are best.	You state and defend your opinions, but you do not make specific references to the research. The committee feels that they need more information before accepting your ideas.	You state your opinions, but you do not defend them. You have not given enough supporting information to make the committee believe that your opinions are valid.
COMPARISON OF ISSUES	You clearly identify commonalities and differences between the issues. The committee gains a thorough understanding of the relationship between the issues.	You identify basic commonalities and differences between the two issues. The committee gains a general idea of the relationship between these issues from your point of view.	You do not identify commonalities or differences between the two issues.
SPEAKING STYLE	Your argument is appropriately tailored to your audience. You use effective vocabulary. Ideas flow smoothly from your introduction to your conclusion. The main idea is evident throughout the argument and is supported by rich detail.	In general, your argument is well tailored to your audience. You have a clear opening statement, argument points, and a conclusion centered on a main idea, although your transitions are choppy.	Your argument is not tailored to the committee's purpose; too many assumptions are made about what the committee knows. A single main idea is difficult to follow in the argument. Supporting details are not provided, making the argument's structure unclear.
PRESENTATION	You are clear and consistent in volume. Your body posture and delivery make it clear that you know your facts, lending credibility to your opinion.	You are believable in your role at times. However, it is sometimes hard to hear you, giving the impression that you are unsure of your opinion.	Your speech is difficult to hear due to volume and/or pace, and it is hard to believe your opinion due to lack of conviction.

These prompts and rubrics were based on the work of Drs. Moon, Brighton, Callahan, and Tomlinson under the Educational Research and Development Centers PR/Award Number R206R50001. All rights permission secured.

Name:_____ Date: _____

ARGUMENT OUTLINE

ASSERTION/OPENING STATEMENT
_____
_____
_____
_____
_____

REASONING # _____
(Circle one)

Cause and Effect   Example   Analogy   Costs vs. Benefits

_____
_____
_____
_____
_____

REASONING # _____
(Circle one)

Cause and Effect   Example   Analogy   Costs vs. Benefits

_____
_____
_____
_____
_____

Name: _____ Date: _____

ARGUMENT OUTLINE

EVIDENCE FOR REASONING # _____

_____

_____

_____

_____

_____

EVIDENCE FOR REASONING # _____

_____

_____

_____

_____

_____

CONCLUSION/CLOSING STATEMENT

_____

_____

_____

_____

_____

_____

_____

_____

What's Your Opinion? © Prufrock Press Inc.

Permission is granted to photocopy or reproduce this page for single classroom use only.

127

ARGUMENT CARDS

ASSERTION
This is what I believe to be true:

_____

_____

_____

_____

_____

_____

_____

_____

ASSERTION
This is what I believe to be true:

_____

_____

_____

_____

_____

_____

_____

_____

ARGUMENT CARDS

REASONING
Costs vs. Benefits

_____

_____

_____

_____

_____

_____

_____

_____

_____

REASONING
Costs vs. Benefits

_____

_____

_____

_____

_____

_____

_____

_____

_____

ARGUMENT CARDS

REASONING
Cause and Effect

_____

_____

_____

_____

_____

_____

_____

_____

REASONING
Cause and Effect

_____

_____

_____

_____

_____

_____

_____

_____

ARGUMENT CARDS

REASONING
Analogy

_____

_____

_____

_____

_____

_____

_____

_____

REASONING
Analogy

_____

_____

_____

_____

_____

_____

_____

_____

ARGUMENT CARDS

REASONING
Example

_____

_____

_____

_____

_____

_____

_____

_____

_____

REASONING
Example

_____

_____

_____

_____

_____

_____

_____

_____

_____

ARGUMENT CARDS

EVIDENCE

_____

_____

_____

_____

_____

_____

_____

_____

EVIDENCE

_____

_____

_____

_____

_____

_____

_____

_____

ARGUMENT CARDS

CONCLUSION

_____

_____

_____

_____

_____

_____

_____

_____

_____

CONCLUSION

_____

_____

_____

_____

_____

_____

_____

_____

_____

What's Your Opinion? © Prufrock Press Inc.

Lesson 8

Concepts
- Internet research
- Citing sources

Materials
- Structure of Debate sheet (p. 138)
- Keyword Search sheet (p. 139)
- Citing Sources sheet (p. 140)

Student Objective
The student demonstrates the ability to conduct research and to cite sources appropriately by using the materials provided (or alternative materials).

Introduction
Demonstrate appropriate research techniques for the medium being used (either Internet or library sources). Then, model an appropriate citation style, either by using the provided Citing Sources sheet or using your preferred style guide.

Recognition
Students complete the Keyword Search sheet.

Application
Students complete the research phase of preparing for the upcoming debate.
1. Students conduct a search for the evidence they need to support their assertions and reasoning.
2. They may use the media center facility or another approved search engine, or you can decide the guidelines for how they are to conduct research.

3. Be sure to be clear about how they should document their sources, how many they need, what appropriate sources look like, and so forth.

Problem Solving

Students should meet in their teams and discuss their arguments.

1. Students should share their research findings and decide which characters should use which information to create the best effect.
2. Students should determine whether they have holes in their arguments that merit more research.

Grade-Level Expectations

The student:

- Identifies potential sources of information.
- Evaluates the relevance of presented information.
- Gathers, organizes, analyzes, and interprets the information.
- Uses evidence to support conclusions.

Additional Notes

- The research component of this unit can be handled in several different ways. You may choose to allow students to use the topics provided and assign them certain websites to use as resources, thus minimizing the time they spend researching their assigned topics. Conversely, you may choose to spend extra time developing their research skills and build in a few extra days for them to do more thorough, independent research.
- Because this is a unit, rather than an entire course of study, we have not included guidance regarding research skills or discussions of style under the assumption that you have taught these topics in the past. If you have not, you may need to dedicate more time to preparing students.
- We have taught this unit using Michael Pollan's *The Omnivore's Dilemma* as a companion text and created debate topics centered on environmental concerns. Prior to having students read the book, we randomly assigned them to pro and con sides of topics relating to the environment and vegetarianism. They did research on these topics for the debate, which resulted in their possessing a more thorough understanding of Pollan's subjects, including the effect of corn production on the environment and the dead zone in the Gulf of Mexico. Also, this structure enabled us to create a classroom file of research articles, which students used while they were preparing for the debate.
- Any grading you do of students' research should be based on some sort of standard with regard to format and style. We recommend that you be very explicit with your expectations for students in terms of the extent of their

research and how they should cite their sources. We have provided a Citing Sources sheet, but you chould adapt this for your students. Many schools have preferred styles. If your school uses a certain style, then we recommend that you make your own style guide showing the parts of a citation, including examples.

STRUCTURE OF DEBATE

PRO	**FIRST ASSERTION** The proposition (the pro side) introduces its assertion. Each of the stakeholders' viewpoints should be represented. **Time limit: 5 minutes**
CON	**FIRST ASSERTION** The opposition (the con side) introduces its assertion. Each of the stakeholders' viewpoints should be represented. **Time limit: 5 minutes**
PRO	**REFUTATION AND REASSERTION** The proposition (the pro side) has the opportunity to present reasoning and evidence to refute the opposition and to support its own assertion. **Time limit: 5 minutes**
CON	**REFUTATION AND REASSERTION** The opposition (the con side) has the opportunity to present reasoning and evidence to refute the opposition side and to support its own assertion. **Time limit: 5 minutes**
CON	**FINAL SUMMARY** The opposition (the con side) has a final opportunity to sum up its arguments, being sure to represent all of the stakeholders' viewpoints. **Time limit: 3 minutes**
PRO	**FINAL SUMMARY** The proposition (the pro side) has a final opportunity to sum up its arguments, being sure to represent all of the stakeholders' viewpoints. **Time limit: 3 minutes**

Name:_____ Date: _____

KEYWORD SEARCH

Step 1: Identify your research topic. (For example, "Including females in the military has had a positive impact.")

My research topic is . . . _____

_____

_____

Step 2: Identify your major concepts. (For example, "female" and "military.")

My two major concepts are . . .

1. _____
2. _____

Step 3: Develop synonymous keywords related to your major concepts. (For example, "woman" and "girl" for "female," and "soldier" and "army" for "military.")

Synonyms for first major concept:

1. _____
2. _____
3. _____

Synonyms for second major concept:

1. _____
2. _____
3. _____

Step 4: Insert Boolean operators such as "AND," "OR," and "NOT."

*   If you want to see sources that involve both words, insert "AND" into your keyword search (for example, type "female AND military").
*   If you want to see sources that list either one word or the other, insert "OR" into your keyword search (for example, type "female OR woman AND military").
*   If you want to exclude certain combinations of words, insert the word "NOT" into your keyword search (for example, type "female OR woman AND military NOT submarines").

My keyword search options are . . .

1. _____
2. _____
3. _____

CITING SOURCES

Book
Author Last Name, First Name. *Title of Book.* Place of publication: Publisher, Copyright date.

Encyclopedia Entry
Author Last Name, First Name. "Article Title." *Title of Encyclopedia.* Edition. Year.

Magazine Article
Author Last Name, First Name. "Article Title." *Title of Magazine,* date of magazine: page(s).

Internet Site
Site Contributor/Creator Last Name, First Name. Title of Site. Date of last update. Address/URL of site.

EBSCO article
Author's Name. "Title of Article." Title of Magazine. Date of issue: page(s). Title of Database. Name of Service. Name of Library. Date of access. URL for homepage of service.

Lesson 9

Concepts
- Synthesizing research
- Self-evaluation

Materials
- Final debate rubrics (pp. 124–125)
- Evaluation sheet (p. 143)
- Post-Unit Activity sheet (p. 144)
- Pretest/posttest rubric (p. 22)

Student Objective

The student demonstrates the ability to organize the parts of an argument and synthesize research by producing a united front with his or her team for a debate.

Introduction

Prior to the debate, meet with each debate team to review its work to date and to make recommendations for the improvement of final preparations.

Recognition

Each team assigns tasks to its members.

Application

Students complete tasks to ensure that they are prepared for the upcoming debate.
1. Students organize their notes and cards for easy retrieval.
2. Students reflect on their word choices, reasoning, and evidence, making sure that their arguments are as strong as possible and modifying them.
3. Students summarize their arguments in their conclusions.

Problem Solving

Students practice for the upcoming debate and then stage debates with opposing teams.

1. Students rehearse debating techniques within their teams.
2. They should pay particular attention to projection and enunciation, organization of their notes, and the team members' strategies for helping one another during the debate.
3. For the debates, be sure that students stick to the provided debate structure.
4. After each debate, the students should be given the opportunity to debrief.

Grade-Level Expectations

The student:

*   Selects appropriate words or explains the use of words in context, including content-specific vocabulary, words with multiple meanings, and precise vocabulary.
*   Exhibits logical organization and uses language appropriate for audience, context, and purpose.
*   Includes smooth transitions, supports thesis with well-chosen details, and provides a coherent conclusion.
*   Uses a variety of strategies of address (e.g., eye contact, speaking rate, volume, articulation, inflection, intonation, rhythm, gesture).

Additional Notes

*   We have found that it is best to score the students as they are debating. This generally results in the most accurate grading. Simply use a highlighter and mark the boxes on the rubric that correspond to student performance. For grading purposes and consistency, you should decide on ranges of point values to be represented by each box and then be sure that where you put your highlighter score indicates how many points a student should receive (e.g., marking the middle of a box signifying a range of 16–20 points would indicate a score of 18).
*   Each debate will take a minimum of 20–25 minutes. We recommend that you allow time to debrief after each debate, although this is up to you. Be sure to steer any discussion in a positive, constructive direction.
*   It is useful to administer the same activity students did in Lesson 1 as a posttest in order to monitor students' knowledge and progression. We have reformatted the pretest as a posttest, but you can use the same rubric provided with Lesson 1.

EVALUATION

PRO	**FIRST ASSERTION**
CON	**FIRST ASSERTION**
PRO	**REFUTATION AND REASSERTION**
CON	**REFUTATION AND REASSERTION**
CON	**FINAL SUMMARY**
PRO	**FINAL SUMMARY**

POST-UNIT ACTIVITY

Using extra paper if necessary, write everything you know about what is included in a debate and in what order a debate takes place. Use as many of the following words as you can.

Analogy	Argument	Assertion
Cause and effect	Conclusion	Cost and benefits
Debate	Evidence	Example
Fallacies	Give and take	Opposition
Proposition	Reasoning	Refutation

A debate is . . . _____

_____

_____

_____

_____

_____

_____

_____

_____

_____

_____

_____

_____

_____

_____

_____

Appendix
Student Context Rubric

The Student Context Rubric (SCR) is intended for use by the classroom teacher as a tool to help in the identification of students of masked potential. This term, *masked potential*, refers to students who are gifted, but are frequently not identified because their behaviors are not displayed to best advantage by traditional methods. The SCR was designed to be used with this series of units and the authentic performance assessments that accompany them. Although you may choose to run the units without using the SCR, you may find the rubric helpful for keeping records of student behaviors.

The units serve as platforms for the display of student behaviors, while the SCR is an instrument that teachers can use to record those behaviors when making observations. The rubric requires the observer to record the frequency of gifted behaviors, but there is also the option to note that the student demonstrates the behavior with particular intensity. In this way, the rubric is subjective and requires careful observation and consideration.

It is recommended that an SCR be completed for each student prior to the application of a unit, and once again upon completion of the unit. In this way, teachers will be reminded of behaviors to look for during the unit—particularly those behaviors that we call *loophole behaviors*, which may indicate giftedness but are often misinterpreted or overlooked. (For instance, a student's verbal ability can be missed if he or she uses it to spin wild lies about having neglected to complete an assignment.) Therefore, the SCR allows teachers to be aware of—and to document—high-ability behavior even if it is masked or used in nontraditional ways. The mechanism also provides a method for tracking changes in teachers' perceptions of their students, not only while students are working on the Interactive Discovery-Based Units for High-Ability Learners, but also while they are engaged in traditional classroom activities.

In observing student behaviors, you might consider some of the following questions after completing a lesson:

- Was there anyone or anything that surprised you today?
- Did a particular student jump out at you today?
- Did someone come up with a unique or unusual idea today?
- Was there a moment in class today when you saw a lightbulb go on? Did it involve an individual, a small group, or the class as a whole?
- In reviewing written responses after a class discussion, were you surprised by anyone (either because he or she was quiet during the discussion but had good written ideas, or because he or she was passionate in the discussion but did not write with the same passion)?
- Did any interpersonal issues affect the classroom today? If so, how were these issues resolved?
- Did the lesson go as planned today? Were there any detours?
- Is there a student whom you find yourself thinking or worrying about outside of school?
- Are there students in your classroom who seem to be on a rollercoaster of learning—"on" one day, but "off" the next?
- Are your students different outside of the classroom? In what ways are they different?
- Are there students who refuse to engage with the project?
- During a class performance, did the leadership of a group change when students got in front of their peers?
- Did your students generate new ideas today?
- What was the energy like in your class today? Did you provide the energy, or did the students?
- How long did it take the students to engage today?

Ideally, multiple observers complete the SCR for each student. If a gifted and talented specialist is available, we recommend that he or she assist. By checking off the appropriate marks to describe student behaviors, and by completing the scoring chart, participants generate quantifiable data that can be used in advocating for students who would benefit from scaffolded services. **In terms of students' scores on the SCR, we do not provide concrete cutoffs or point requirements regarding which students should be recommended for special services.** Rather, the SCR is intended to flag students for scaffolded services and to enable them to reach their potential. It also provides a way to monitor and record students' behaviors.

What follows is an explanation of the categories and items included on the SCR, along with some examples of how the specified student behaviors might be evidenced in your classroom.

Engagement

1. **Student arrives in class with new ideas to bring to the project that he or she has thought of outside of class.** New ideas may manifest themselves as ideas about how to approach a problem, about new research information found on the Internet or elsewhere outside of class, about something in the news or in the paper that is relevant to the subject, or about a connection between the subject and an observed behavior.

2. **Student shares ideas with a small group of peers, but may fade into the background in front of a larger group.** The student may rise to be a leader when the small group is working on a project, but if asked to get up in front of the class, then that student fades into the background and lets others do the talking.

3. **Student engagement results in a marked increase in the quality of his or her performance.** This is particularly evident in a student who does not normally engage in class at all. During the unit, the student suddenly becomes engaged and produces something amazing.

4. **Student eagerly interacts with appropriate questions, but may be reluctant to put things down on paper.** This is an example of a loophole behavior, or one that causes a student to be overlooked when teachers and specialists are identifying giftedness. It is particularly evident in students who live in largely "oral" worlds, which is to say that they communicate best verbally and are often frustrated by written methods, or in those who have writing disabilities.

Creativity

1. **Student intuitively makes "leaps" in his or her thinking.** Occasionally, you will be explaining something, and a lightbulb will go on for a student, causing him or her to take the concept far beyond the content being covered. Although there are students who do this with regularity, it is more often an intensity behavior, meaning that when it occurs, the student is very intense in his or her thinking, creativity, reasoning, and so on. This can be tricky to identify, because often, the student is unable to explain his or her thinking, and the teacher realizes only later that a leap in understanding was achieved.

2. **Student makes up new rules, words, or protocols to express his or her own ideas.** This can take various forms, one of which is a student's taking two words and literally combining them to try to express what he or she is thinking about. Other times, a student will want to change the rules to make his or her idea possible.

3. **Student thinks on his or her feet in response to a project challenge, to make excuses, or to extend his or her work.** This is another loophole

behavior, because it often occurs when a student is being defensive or even misbehaving, making a teacher less likely to interpret it as evidence of giftedness. It is sometimes on display during classroom debates and discussions.

4. **Student uses pictures or other inventive means to illustrate his or her ideas.** Given the choice, this student would rather draw an idea than put it into words. This could take the shape of the student creating a character web or a design idea. The student might also act out an idea or use objects to demonstrate understanding.

Synthesis

1. **Student goes above and beyond directions to expand ideas.** It is wonderful to behold this behavior in students, particularly when displayed by those students who are rarely engaged. A student may be excited about a given idea and keep generating increasingly creative or complex material to expand upon that idea. For instance, we had a student who, during the mock trial unit, became intrigued by forensic evidence and decided to generate and interpret evidence to bolster his team's case.

2. **Student has strong opinions on projects, but may struggle to accept directions that contradict his or her opinions.** This student may understand directions, but be unwilling to yield to an idea that conflicts with his or her own idea. This behavior, rather than indicating a lack of understanding, is typical of students with strong ideas.

3. **Student is comfortable processing new ideas.** This behavior is evident in students who take new ideas and quickly extend them or ask insightful questions.

4. **Student blends new and old ideas.** This behavior has to do with processing a new idea, retrieving an older idea, and relating the two to one another. For instance, a student who learns about using string to measure distance might remember making a treasure map and extrapolate that a string would have been useful for taking into account curves and winding paths.

Interpersonal Ability

1. **Student is an academic leader who, when engaged, increases his or her levels of investment and enthusiasm in the group.** This is a student who has so much enthusiasm for learning that he or she makes the project engaging for the whole group, fostering an attitude of motivation or optimism.

2. **Student is a social leader in the classroom, but may not be an academic leader.** To observe this type of behavior, you may have to be vigilant, for some students are disengaged in the classroom but come alive as soon as they cross the threshold into the hallway, where they can socialize with their

peers. Often, this student is able to get the rest of the group to do whatever he or she wants (and does not necessarily use this talent for good).

3. **Student works through group conflict to enable the group to complete its work.** When the group has a conflict, this is the student who solves the problem or addresses the issue so that the group can get back to work. This is an interpersonal measure, and thus, it does not describe a student who simply elects to do all of the work rather than confronting his or her peers about sharing the load.

4. **Student is a Tom Sawyer in classroom situations, using his or her charm to get others to do the work.** There is an important distinction to watch out for when identifying this type of behavior: You must be sure that the student is *not* a bully, coercing others to do his or her work. Instead, this student actually makes other students *want* to lend a helping hand. For instance, a twice-exceptional student who is highly talented but struggles with reading might develop charm in order to get other students to transpose his verbally expressed ideas into writing.

Verbal Communication

1. **Participation in brainstorming sessions (e.g., group work) increases student's productivity.** When this type of student is given the opportunity to verbally process with peers, he or she is often able to come up with the answer. For instance, if asked outright for an answer, this student may shrug, but if given a minute to consult with a neighbor, then the student usually is able and willing to offer the correct answer.

2. **Student constructively disagrees with peers and/or the teacher by clearly sharing his or her thoughts.** This student can defend his or her point of view with examples and reasoning—not just in a formal debate, but also in general classroom situations. He or she has learned to channel thoughts into constructive disagreement, rather than flying off the handle merely to win an argument.

3. **Student verbally expresses his or her academic and/or social needs.** This student can speak up when confused or experiencing personality clashes within a group. This student knows when to ask for help and can clearly articulate what help is needed.

4. **Student uses strong word choice and a variety of tones to bring expression to his or her verbal communication.** This student is an engaging speaker and speaks loudly and clearly enough for everybody to hear. A wide vocabulary is also indicative that this student's verbal capability is exceptional.

Student: _____

Date: _____

Fill out the rubric according to what you have observed about each student's behaviors. Then, for each area, record the number of items you marked "Not observed," "Sometimes," and "Often." Multiply these tallies by the corresponding point values (0, 1, and 2) to get the totals for each area. There is an option to check for high intensity so you can better keep track of students' behaviors.

STUDENT CONTEXT RUBRIC

ENGAGEMENT

1. Student arrives in class with new ideas to bring to the project that he or she has thought of outside of class.
   NOT OBSERVED   SOMETIMES   OFTEN   HIGH INTENSITY

2. Student shares ideas with a small group of peers, but may fade into the background in front of a larger group.
   NOT OBSERVED   SOMETIMES   OFTEN   HIGH INTENSITY

3. Student engagement results in a marked increase in the quality of his or her performance.
   NOT OBSERVED   SOMETIMES   OFTEN   HIGH INTENSITY

4. Student eagerly interacts with appropriate questions, but may be reluctant to put things down on paper.
   NOT OBSERVED   SOMETIMES   OFTEN   HIGH INTENSITY

CREATIVITY

1. Student intuitively makes "leaps" in his or her thinking.
   NOT OBSERVED   SOMETIMES   OFTEN   HIGH INTENSITY

2. Student makes up new rules, words, or protocols to express his or her own ideas.
   NOT OBSERVED   SOMETIMES   OFTEN   HIGH INTENSITY

3. Student thinks on his or her feet in response to a project challenge, to make excuses, or to extend his or her work.
   NOT OBSERVED   SOMETIMES   OFTEN   HIGH INTENSITY

4. Student uses pictures or other inventive means to illustrate his or her ideas.
   NOT OBSERVED   SOMETIMES   OFTEN   HIGH INTENSITY

SYNTHESIS

1. Student goes above and beyond directions to expand ideas.
   NOT OBSERVED   SOMETIMES   OFTEN   HIGH INTENSITY

2. Student has strong opinions on projects, but may struggle to accept directions that contradict his or her opinions.
   NOT OBSERVED   SOMETIMES   OFTEN   HIGH INTENSITY

3. Student is comfortable processing new ideas.
   NOT OBSERVED   SOMETIMES   OFTEN   HIGH INTENSITY

4. Student blends new ideas and old ideas.
   NOT OBSERVED   SOMETIMES   OFTEN   HIGH INTENSITY

INTERPERSONAL ABILITY

1. Student is an academic leader who, when engaged, increases his or her levels of investment and enthusiasm in the group.
   NOT OBSERVED   SOMETIMES   OFTEN   HIGH INTENSITY

2. Student is a social leader in the classroom, but may not be an academic leader.
   NOT OBSERVED   SOMETIMES   OFTEN   HIGH INTENSITY

3. Student works through group conflict to enable the group to complete its work.
   NOT OBSERVED   SOMETIMES   OFTEN   HIGH INTENSITY

4. Student is a Tom Sawyer in classroom situations, using his or her charm to get others to do the work.
   NOT OBSERVED   SOMETIMES   OFTEN   HIGH INTENSITY

VERBAL COMMUNICATION

1. Participation in brainstorming sessions (e.g., group work) increases student's productivity.
   NOT OBSERVED   SOMETIMES   OFTEN   HIGH INTENSITY

2. Student constructively disagrees with peers and/or the teacher by clearly sharing his or her thoughts.
   NOT OBSERVED   SOMETIMES   OFTEN   HIGH INTENSITY

3. Student verbally expresses his or her academic and/or social needs.
   NOT OBSERVED   SOMETIMES   OFTEN   HIGH INTENSITY

4. Student uses strong word choice and a variety of tones to bring expression to his or her verbal communication.
   NOT OBSERVED   SOMETIMES   OFTEN   HIGH INTENSITY

AREA	NOT 0	SOME 1	OFTEN 2	HIGH	TOTAL
ENGAGEMENT					
CREATIVITY					
SYNTHESIS					
INTERPERSONAL ABILITY					
VERBAL COMMUNICATION					
ADD TOTALS					

Developed by Cote & Blauvelt under the auspices of the Further Steps Forward Project, a Jacob Javits grant program, #S206A050086.

What's Your Opinion? © Prufrock Press Inc.

About the Authors

Richard G. Cote, M.B.A., is a career educator. He has dedicated 41 years to being a classroom teacher (mathematics, physics), a community college adjunct instructor (economics), a gifted and talented resource specialist, and the director of the Further Steps Forward Project, a Javits Grant program.

His development of the MESH (mathematics, English, science, and history) program has led him to several audiences. He has presented at various national conventions, civic/community groups, district school boards, teacher organizations, community colleges, and universities, and has served as a consultant to educators throughout the country. Cote helped develop the teacher certification examination for physics at the Institute for Educational Testing and Research at the University of South Florida. He completed the Florida Council on Educational Management Program in Educational Leadership, and he is the recipient of numerous awards, including a certificate of merit on economics education from the University of South Florida, a grant from the Florida Council on Economics Education, a Florida Compact award, and a prestigious NAGC Curriculum Studies award for the development of *Ecopolis* and *What's Your Opinion?*

Now retired from the workplace, Cote continues to share his energy, creativity, and expertise with educators through the Interactive Discovery-Based Units for High-Ability Learners.

Darcy O. Blauvelt has been teaching in a variety of facilities for more than 12 years. Her educational journey has included public schools, private schools, nursery schools, and a professional theatre for children ages 3–18. Blauvelt holds educational certification in Theatre K–12, Early Childhood Education, and English Education 5–12. She holds a B.A. in theatre from Chatham College, Pittsburgh, PA, and has done graduate work at Lesley University in Massachusetts in creative arts in learning, as well as at Millersville University in Pennsylvania in psychology.

In 2005, she joined the Nashua School District as a gifted and talented resource specialist. Subsequently, she served full time as the program coordinator for the Further Steps Forward Project, a Javits Grant program, from 2005–2009. Blauvelt returned to the classroom in the fall of 2009 and currently teaches seventh-grade English in Nashua, NH. Blauvelt lives in Manchester, NH with her husband, two dogs, five cats, and the occasional son!